HOMING

The Collected Poems

of Don Welch

1975-2015

Rogue Faculty Press
Ralston, NE

All rights reserved under International and Pan-American Copyright Conventions. No part of this book may be reproduced in any manner whatsoever without written permission from the publisher, except in the case of brief quotations embodied in critical articles and reviews.

Copyright© 2016 by Don Welch
ISBN 978-0-692-71082-1

First Edition

Cover art by Calvin Banks
Author photo by Kat Shiffler/Platte Basin Timelapse

Printed in the USA on acid-free paper.
To order online, go to *amazon.com*.

Table of Contents

INTRODUCTION •

From DEAD HORSE TABLE (1975)

LINES FOR MY FATHER •1
FLAT WATER •2
NORTH AND WEST •3
THE GRACE OF SNAILS •4
ANNA PETRULSKI'S •5
SISTER CONCEPCIOUN •6
THAT RUMOR OF A TRUE LIBERAL ARTIST
    VISITING ME IS ALMOST TRUE •7
BARK •8
SONG FOR A PRIEST
    LEAVING THE CHURCH •9
CARP •10
FUNERAL AT ANSLEY •11

From HANDWORK (1978)

INDIAN SUMMER •12
THE REACHES OF THE PLATTE RIVER •14
THE MYTHOLOGIST •15
HANDWORK •16
FIRST LOVE SONG •17
FOURTH LOVE SONG •18
OLD MARRIAGE FIGURE •19

From THE RARER GAME (1980)

THE RARER GAME: A SEQUENCE OF POEMS
  ABOUT BIRDS AND AN ANIMAL
    1. The Mute Swans •22
    2. The Snow Geese •23
    3. The Bull Elk •24
    4. The Eider •26
    5. The Hawk •27
CARDINAL •28
THE DOE •29
POET IN RESIDENCE AT A
    COUNTRY SCHOOL •30
SINGING A BIRD'S SONG •32
THE RUNNER •34
HOW TO LIVE IN BUFFALO COUNTY •35
FISHING, AT COOT SHALLOWS •36
MY MAD UNCLE'S MAD SONG FOR
    CHRISTMAS •37
THE COYOTE •38
MILE RELAY, 4TH LEG •39
THE SHOTGUN •40
NEBRASKA •41

From THE KEEPER OF MINIATURE DEER (1986)

OLD SUMMERS •42
SMALLEST DAUGHTER •43
COAT-OF-ARMS •44
DOWSER •45
QUIXOTE'S MEDITATIONS ON A PLAIN •46
THE KEEPER OF MINIATURE DEER •47

THE CASTRATUS •48
THE RIVER •49

THE BREEDER OF ARCHANGELS (1991) •51

From THE PLATTE RIVER (1992

NOW, AT THE EDGE OF THIS RIVER •54
WHITE CRANES IN SPRING •55
THE PAINTER AND THE RIVER •56
THE VET •57
THE RIVER AS A FIGURE OF LOVE •58
TELL YOURSELF •59
THE SMALL RELIQUARY •60
RIVER DEER •61
AFTER A BLIZZARD •62
TWO SNAILS •63
THE TALE OF WATER •64

From THE MARGINALIST (1992

THE MARGINALIST •65
NOUNS •66
THE UNICORN •67
SAPPHIRE •69
HOME FROM THE WORD STORE •71
FIRST BOOK APOCRYPHA •72
OLD WOMAN •73
LOT'S WIFE •74
THE CHRISTMAS WREATHER •76

OLD GERMAN WOMAN •77
MY DEAR MISS DICKINSON, •78

From CARVED BY OBADIAH VERITY (1993)

CARVED BY OBADIAH VERITY •80
THE GLASSED BIRD •81
FIVE IRISH PICTURES:

      1. The Glassworker •82
      2. Barley Cove, West Cork •83
      3. Old Men, Aran Islands •84
      4. Stone Rubbing, Dowth Passage Grave •85
      5. The White Deer of Mallow •86

From THE WORDS WHICH MARRY ME TO YOU (1995) •87

From FIRE'S TONGUE IN THE CANDLE'S END (1996)

LETTER TO MY CHILDREN •89
OF NOTE TO A YOUNG WRITER •90
TO A FRIEND STARTING A NEW POETRY JOURNAL •91
LETTER TO PETER •92
TO A BEGINNING POET •94
ABOUT YOUR CLASSROOMS •98

SOME WORDS FOR MY SON,
 A NOVICE HUNTER •99
TO VERN, ABOUT A FLANKER •100
TO A NUDE SUNBATHER •101
THE UNDERTONES •102
THERE IS NO WIND IN HEAVEN •103

From **A BRIEF HISTORY OF**
 FEATHERS (1996)

BALTIMORE ORIOLE •104
BARN OWL •105
THE BROWN GROUSE •106
THE MUTE SWANS •107
TURKEY VULTURE •108
THE DEAD KINGBIRD •109
BLACK TERN •110
THE LAST WILD PASSENGER PIGEON •111
POSTCARD ABOUT A FALCON •112
OSTRICH •113
THE CRANES •114
TO A SPARROW HAWK •116
SCENE I, INVOLVING YOU AND AN OWL •117

From **EVERY MOUTH OF AUTUMN**
 SAYS GOODBYE (1996)•118

CRANES: A BOOK OF HOURS (1996)

MATINS •123
LAUDS •123

PRIME •123
TERCE •124
SEXT •125
NONES •125
VESPERS •126
COMPLINE •126
MATINS •127

From IN THE FIELD'S HANDS (1998)

JANUARY •128
MARCH •129
APRIL •130
SEPTEMBER •131

From THE PLAIN SENSE OF THINGS (1999)

HOME TO YOUR HOME PLACE •132

From INKLINGS (2001)

TWO HORSES •133
DROUGHT •134
THE WILDFIRE •135
AN ACRE OF BUTTERFLIES •136
THE SHUNNING •137
ACROSS THE ROAD FROM
    THE CEMETERY •139

LISTENING TO A PAVANE BY
    GABRIEL FAURE •140
AT THE ROAD'S EDGE •142
THE GEESE •143
THE HIGH JUMPER •144
TO BEAR BRYANT, SOMEWHERE ON THAT
    TALLER TOWER •145
FALL, NEBRASKA •146
A ROUNDBALL HOSANNA •148
THE GRAMMAR OF BRONZE •149
TO A RECLUSIVE PHILOSOPHER •151
INKLINGS •152
A SONG OF WREATHS •153
A BIRTHDAY PRESENT •154
POSTCARDS TO AN APHORIST •155
NEVER WRITE IN A GLASS HOUSE •156

From **THE YARN BIN (2001)**

FOR OUR GRANDDAUGHTER PLAYING IN THE
    SUN •157
"WOMAN ON A VERANDA" •158
THE CRAYON EATER •159
THE BOY •162
GOLD MEDAL WINNER •163
APRIL •165
THE TREEHOUSE •166

From **GUTTER FLOWERS: THE ALLEY
POEMS (2002-2005)**

ALLEYS •168
THE YOUNG WIDOW •169

WHILE LEANING AGAINST A GARBAGE CAN BEHIND THE PRINCE OF PEACE CHURCH •170
MARCH MONDAY •171
ALLEY POET •172
RUNNING OFF •173
WITH FADED EYES AND A DIRTY DRESS •174
BEHIND THE MONUMENT COMPANY •175
CINDERS AND HOLLYHOCKS •176
GUTTER FLOWERS •177
FOR THE BATTERED GIRL WHO ALWAYS SAID HELLO •178
OLD COUPLE, PORCH SCENE •179
A DROP OF DEW •180
FLOWERING PLUM BUSH •181
PENNY ODES •182
TOO COLD •183
INSIDE BLUE'S TAVERN •184
THE MAN WITH A GARDEN FOR A YARD •185
AT THE EDGE OF TOWN •186
AMONG THE POOR •187
AT THE LAST INTERSECTION •188

From WHEN MEMORY GIVES DUST A FACE (2008)

WHEN MEMORY GIVES DUST A FACE •189
LITANY •190
OLD IMMIGRANT •191
AT FOURTEEN •192
OUR ADONIS •193
WALKING WITH MY FATHER'S SHADOW •194
MET SOPRANO •195
ZORN •196

THAT SUMMER •197
THE CONEFLOWER •198
WITH YOU, AMONG THE CHURCH RUINS AT
    DEVENISH, IRELAND •199
ON YOUR BIRTHDAY, REMEMBER •200
JUST BEFORE CHRISTMAS •201
ABOUT EDUCATION •203
CENTENNIAL POEM •204
A REQUIEM FOR A TEACHER,
    STANLEY SMITH •205
DISTANCE •207
DEATH •208
NEAR THE END OF HIS LIFE •209
TO FIND ME •210

From TRAVELS (2010)

THE PROMPTING OF A POEM •211
TO A CARDINAL •212
ELEGY FOR THE END OF MOTION •213
LYMAN LAKE, ARIZONA •214
MONTANA SKY •215
AFTER HAYING •216
IN TURNER'S FIELD •217
WHEN THAT SNOW DIED •218
FROM A VILLAGE IN NORMANDY •219
FROM TUSCANY •220
JUNE, DENALI PARK, ALASKA •221
BELFAST •222
DUBLIN •223

From DELIBERATIONS (2012)

TO REMIND MYSELF •224

WHAT IS A GOOD ROOM •225
REFLECTIONS, BEGINNING WITH TERNS •226
GRACE •228
From TRYING TO REMEMBER LI PO •229
A SCRIBE •232
THE ART DECOY •233
THE GLASSBLOWER •234
THE BUILDER AND THE SINGER •235
IN OLD TOWN, A TRIPLET •236
LOOKING AT AN OLD PHOTO, THROUGH SEPIA •238
AMONG THE THINGS THAT DARKENED THAT EVENING •239
IN HIS HAILED-OUT GREENHOUSE •240
MOWING •241
From ENDINGS •242

IN TIMES OF CONSIDERABLE WARS and INTERLUDES (2013)

    1st Interlude •245
NEAR THE END OF OUR LONG WAR •246
    2nd Interlude •247
    3rd Interlude •248
FROM THE CHRONICLES •249
    4th Interlude •253
    5th Interlude •254
AFTER THE BODY BAG •255
    6th Interlude •256
IN A DEATH CAMP'S MUSEUM •257
    7th Interlude •258
UPON THE ARRIVAL OF THE REFUGEES •259
    8th Interlude •260
FROM KOSOVO •261
    9th Interlude •262

YOUR VICTIM •263
   10th Interlude •264
LETTER TO AANYA, TWO MONTHS
   OLD, IN ISLAMABAD •265
   11th Interlude •267
IN A TIME OF CONSIDERABLE WARS

1. *The Corporal* •*268*
2. *For Those in the Lame Man Platoon* •*268*
3. *Overcast* •*269*
4. *In This Hole in the Earth* •*269*
5. *New Snow* •*270*

From GNOMES (2013) •272

From MORNING: LAST POEMS (2014)

ON THE WAY TO SCHOOL •277
WITH GOOD MUSIC IN MY HEAD •288
YOUNG •289
FOR THE KID STILL DELIVERING THE
   GOODS •290
FOR SHIRLEY BUETTNER •291
THE IRIS •292
THE WHITE BLACKBIRD •293
AFTER THE SUICIDE BOMBING •294
THIS MORNING •285
AFTER ALL THESE YEARS •286
SILENCE, AGAIN •287
THE PERFECT •288

From THE KEEPERS' PILE (2015)

IN THE DUCK BLIND •289
ROWE SANCTUARY •290
PHEBE •291
JACK'S LAST NOTES TO JILL •292
THE WORD IS NOT FREE •293
RELOADING SHELLS •294

AUTHOR'S ACKNOWLEDGMENTS •297

EDITOR'S ACKNOWLEDGMENTS •298

INTRODUCTION

After forty years practicing his art, the subject of Don Welch's early poem "The Glassworker" is not satisfied. He cradles whiskey in his strong hands and concludes, "I want purer." In one of the happier instances of art imitating life and vice versa, this collection represents forty years in the career of a poet. In these pages, the reader will find Welch saying again and again that he, too, wants purer.

Welch, longtime Nebraska poet, teacher, and racer of homing pigeons, is in many ways similar to his own glassworker. His glassworker knows well "the way / the rigor held, then softened. . . ." Anyone who comes to Welch's poetry for the first time through this volume will find it initially very rigorous, created by a strong intellectual who has read (to use his phrase) the long shelf of poetry as thoroughly as a person can. That said, the poems' rigor immediately softens into readability, "spun into iridescences by line, / tone, the elements of love." In other words, the poetry of Don Welch has a wide academic foreground, but a reader needs no other academic degree to read it well except a reverence for nature, tradition, family, words, and—above all—craft.

As for subjects, Welch's poems draw extensively from the natural world. Rivers flow through or nearby most every poem of the collection, while birds of all species fly overhead and animals move along the periphery. Even poems set indoors read as if they have just arrived from outside. For Welch, poetry is an outdoor sport. At the same time, so many aspects of the human world arise in the poetry as well—people at their best, for instance in marriage, music, and sports; and at their worst, in exploitation, hatred, and warfare.

Welch's work knows both scope and precision. Like his pigeons, the poems travel far, then home in.

Thus, the title of this extended selection of Welch's four decades of poetry is *Homing*. It aims to be a generous sampling of the over two dozen books Welch has published, some of which are not readily available, if at all, to the reading public. The publisher, Rogue Faculty Press, works independently, highlighting the works of teachers who create. Welch is an absolute model of such a teacher, whose individual craft heightened his classroom work while his classroom work kept his individual craft accessible and, yes, even practical.

Teaching, as with any art, can instill both confidence and humility simultaneously. As Welch's glassworker might put it in regard to his own practice,

> I know I'm good, he said,
> but let's say in that moment
> between my death and fame
> there might be something light-caught,
> pure, undreamed--even
> crystalline with good oblivion . . .(82)

The persistent practice of an art allows a person to see, via the art, beyond that art. In his classrooms Welch showed thousands of students how to make the white space after a well-made poem resonate with meaning. Over and over again in the following poems, Welch is still demonstrating how to use words to attain to wordlessness.

Their cumulative effect, though, is even higher and greater. What is the white space beyond the white space? The glassworker envisions for himself a purity like this . . . "then, aware of the absurdity, / he laughed."

Nevertheless, for four decades the poetry of Don Welch has always been homing in on the purer. We may never get there, we teachers and writers, but God forbid if we don't try. And begin again. And keep going.

—D.S.

*I loved good works
    because they cleansed the air between them.*

*The air for me
    was such a generous house.*

From DEAD HORSE TABLE (1975)

LINES FOR MY FATHER

I love you, old man, in our time.
The shotgun cradled in your arm,
the marbled wood,
the varnished sky.

The milo's cut.
The fence holds leaves.
The thicket has its quail
and the final green.

We walk.
We clot in time.
The fence sings birdless
in the wind.

FLAT WATER

Coming down to the river is no wish
to see its liquid tin in the sun.
It's a wanting to smell it, a wanting
to test the old sense which pulls you on.

That's why you take the brush slowly
as a game. You remember the boys already there,
the boys diving in it, laughing at the wet cats
of their heads. That's why you think out loud,

Watch out for too much shallow, the rash
of salt-shot. And you hear girls dancing in it,
daring it to crawl higher than permission.
You feel them giggle at the soft clamps

the Platte puts to them. But you stop
50 yards from the bank, listening to underground
water. Finding its way articled, it spreads out,
spreads down. You hear rich muted fossils,

the dark entertainment. You hear your youngest
coming back with the Platte in her hands.
You hear her laugh the bank, play the small carp
in the buckbrush. Even before she gets to you,

you say, Here comes trip's truth in small ends.
What kind of gladness is this, then, when you find
she's cupped so hard no river's left?

NORTH AND WEST

The places you shot pheasants
are there. Harrows weeds
are hiding, the slough at
the outskirts of North Akron.
When you turn the section line
west of Primrose, you can think
anything, but there it is:
the weeds and hills draw down
to the road's edge, and your eyes
going out to whatever season
meet at a place they set aside
in the talk of shots,
the ambivalence of dead birds.

THE GRACE OF SNAILS

They are here,
slugged slick with belief,
true to the pale edges they slide out after.

They, too, move beyond knowing.
They hazard eyes, hoping wan convoluted tongues
will follow.

Born to jellies,
what would they be without mud?
Or beyond the pectins of some birds?

They lisp silently under broad leaves,
daily of lilies. At night they put eyes
back in their heads.

But were they to rest upon a human finger or
anything lighter than the stones which
grouse them, not even then

would they hymn themselves good fortune.
They have a capacity to stay.
There, small-bunged, they chew shade

and sing a white tactile music,
self-dimensioning,
arranged.

ANNA PETRULSKI'S

a white bat, has a kind face,
and is nurse of nobody else.

I never see her leave her house,
enter her Plymouth.

I never see her buckle her girth's membrane
(or for that matter,

starch her duty).
She simply flies, true to traffic,

and settles among whatever trees
benignly bloom in the parking lot.

Gets out, is exorcised until
she's so smooth the dooms of history

can't hang from the old points of her
elbows. Backs in, sits down,

and while moving past my forehead into my eyes
gives me an inverted smile, a breve, a hover;

then drops her hand's great flange,
broad as the edge of ether.

SISTER CONCEPCIOUN

Sister, I must tell you,
in your new habit and from the rear
you look like a casaba melon

(my favorite of all those things that
snaked along the ground in Eden).
And I thought you'd be the first to change.

I remember when you were a patch of
snow in one fall's leaves—the greens, reds,
golds, and browns of summered legs.

A winter ptarmigan, you brooded your thought
through all my sophomores. How does one
blend her habit with the leaves of grass?

you asked,
your reverential mask made comic
by a carbonated wit.

And after class we talked parochial,
of St. Teresa, Catherine of Siena,
and a Whitman whose christian name is Walt.

THAT RUMOR OF A TRUE LIBERAL ARTIST
VISITING ME IS ALMOST TRUE

On brown toothpicks
the wasp approaches
the clear pane of glass,
and as if married to
a denser sense, turns
at a right angle and
takes the old wood
to the ceiling.

There he stops,
his fuselage moving
in and out, waxing
the instinct which
got him there
in the first place.

At length he grows
contemplative. He
lets the brown bands
of his abdomen loop
whatever's yellow.

In the mean time
three leaves fall
peripherally through
a thousand running feet
of air, and the dry nectar
of vocations passes over
him before he toothpicks
into whatever's later
and is gone.

BARK

Useless to ask what this was
before it crusted. It has the face
of Frost over Auden. But it doesn't
worry. It takes itself in folds.

Ants climb it because it's theirs.
Beetles hide in it because it's fun
to tease beginning peckers. Adult
peckers are something else again.

Aphids know this, and so they sneak
out at dark to dibble in its wounds.
But the only things bark doesn't love
are leaves and lightning.

The goddamned leaves think bark's a scab.
They're always picking at it with their fingers,
thinking if the edge came off they'd feel
a flush dying into life.

But they just dull their edges, and bark
sends them messages of oriental consolation.
You can always tell when the messages
come through. Leaves' mouths

grow frenetic, and they defend
the beauty of their multifoliate existence.
Bark just trunk-chuckles, and occasionally
cuts off their sap.

SONG FOR A PRIEST LEAVING THE CHURCH

Let there be praise
for the clear water
of music just below
the level of your ear

which runs ahead
involving itself
and springing into
the distance;

and if it stops by
a quizzical tree
and goes round and through
the stained worlds of grass,

let it be as sure
as relief in the sense
of its giving—and
as tactless as noses

in taking whatever is
near for its course.

CARP

In water they look huge.
They sabotage the sand
around submerged timber until
the pilings of the dock lose
their attention.

But they take no bait. Instead,
they chew their yellow mouths
or gulp hunks of invisible liver
in old car bodies.

After lunch they loom six feet below
the surface, their enzymes
running.

God, what backs, we say.
They eat our eyes, we say.
Otherwise, they hump,
scabbarded, dun-tongued.

And when their moss sides start
to roach and their sag bellies jiggle
and pull in—when they finally squirt
as if split into needle-nose gar,
we discover it's illusory,
wind across water.

At evening they come up,
their eyes so full of ordnance
we expect them to attack the air,
but they don't. They just lip
the top, and a pale satisfaction
circles out of them and fills
the county.

FUNERAL AT ANSLEY

I write of a cemetery,
of the perpetual care of buffalo grass,
of kingbirds and catbirds
and cottonwoods;

of wild roses around headstones,
with their high thin stems
and their tight tines
and their blooms pursed
in the morning.

I write of old faces,
of cotton hose and flowered dresses
and mouths which have grown up
on the weather.

And I write of one woman
who lies a last time in the long sun
of August, uncramped by the wind
which autumns each one of us

under catbirds and kingbirds
and cottonwoods, and the gray-green
leaves of the buffalo grass.

From HANDWORK (1978)

INDIAN SUMMER

Somehow it is never hard work
to mourn well in October,
Indian summer being a time
of easy mourning.

We remember the smell
of leaves burning, the smoke
drifting over the fields,
angels of wood.

In October the moon, hanging,
always comes down a little,
and a woman almost forms,
then forms just below the hills.

As if she is holding out something,
as if what she holds
smells of sage and corn,
and she's coming up toward the house.

And somehow we feel
we have always known her.
In a gourd cup she carries
the moon, there is a musk

on her dried flowers,
the moments of her voice
hang down like grapes.
And since we are alone

we can suffer such sentiment,
here in the twilight, the road
past our house a long door
asking us in.

THE REACHES OF THE PLATTE RIVER

Out here distance
runs on to the reaches.

Past the heron
moving its peculiar gray
through morning,
past the crane
in its slow glimmer
in the light.

Only up close
is the eye exact,
and then things run on.

And unlike the killdeer
the reaches camouflage themselves
in themselves.

So we say
there are moments
in which dares, like hunters,
shatter space.

In which love, unopened,
is still conclusion.

But neither of these
describes the way
we go into the reaches.

To go deep into what they are
we fly as silently as owls,
the wind pushing our soft masks back.

THE MYTHOLOGIST

Because it was too dark
to finish mowing,
he went inside
and told his wife
he had something
trapped in the last
standing grass.

My little heroic gesture
he laughed,
to a corn-wolf
or plant-fox
or something.

But that night,
as he dreamed of cutting
the final swath,
what flew out
at the last moment looked
for all the world like a
navel-string.

And after it
the only child he would
never have.

HANDWORK

We found these things,
we rubbed them down
until their grains shone.

What was left
we looked at hard,
until the vaults in them
ran off like lines in rocks.

Until we were too broad
to follow.

So there were times
when we came out of them
like miners into the sun,
carrying only black centers
in our eyes.

But there were also times when
we knew where we'd been;
we knew by what
we held in our hands.

Which we kept putting down
on the tables of our wives.

FIRST LOVE SONG

It's raining: the language
of this place is taking a shower.

As soon as a noun's out it's washed,
and if you watch closely enough

it sits on a wire, preening,
putting itself in place.

It's crazy, I know, but after
its head dips under its wing,

its mouth brings a syllable up,
stretches it like a small bow,

and verbs follow like arrows.
And when they fly into trees,

landing between thorns,
it's that kind of day.

They perch there, sound wet,
kissing themselves.

And to you, I say this
at the risk of your confusion:

I cannot love you
as I love you in this poem.

FOURTH LOVE SONG

It is cold.
The wind cutting through
the side of the house
is entering the kitchen
at our knees.

As you spoon
loose tea into your cup,
your hands are a blend
of everything I love.

Large, full of descriptions,
full of small stories.

And the small ring
on your finger? How long
was it before I grew up
to the double truth of the years,
that small rings, just right,
are all wrong for some hands?

In the late afternoon
the icicles have stopped growing
from the eaves, their tips
faint with a yellow silence.

I watch you wrap your hands
around your tea cup.
Under the cold porcelain surface
a warm bone sings.

OLD MARRIAGE FIGURE

> —*Poetry always remembers its roots in primitive culture.*
>
> *Jerome Rothenberg*

And he will say:

> You are two small things.
> You are corners of time wrapped by two eyes
> and two hands and minds tied to local
> attention.
> Give me your roots.

And the man and the woman
will take from their lives roots for the occasion.
And the roots will be split at one end,
and two eyes will appear at the other end,
and strings will run through the eyes of the roots
and around the couple's necks.

And he will say:

> This is man and woman.
> They are as different as fire and river,
> as similar as the hedge apple
> and the heart-shaped linden.
> Take them into the circle.
> I will marry their roots.

And he will take the woman's root
with its red thread,
and he will take the man's root
that hangs from his string,
and he will sew their roots together.

And he will say:

> Bring forth a widow
> and let her bless these roots.

And a widow will come forth carrying desire.
She will touch the roots until they know
what absence is.

And he will say:

> Bring forth dead who knew what love was.
> Let them move past this couple and into the
>   trees,
> and let the trees move.

Then he will ask:

> Who has the sacred voice?

And a child will bring him one of her words.

And he will say:

> I release this voice.
> Let it dance in the circle.

And the voice will shatter the air with light.
It will move over the short-grass,
wrinkling it with fire.

And the old man will wait.
He will wait until the voice draws back
before he says:

There is only one fear in the world.
We believe we lose ourselves
by losing anything we love.

From THE RARER GAME (1980)

THE RARER GAME: A SEQUENCE OF POEMS ABOUT BIRDS AND AN ANIMAL

1. The Mute Swans

A sign on the park fence told us what they were:
Mute Swans, Origin England,
Weight Exceeding Fifteen Pounds.

They swam alone, unreeling our attention.

With their rinds of feathers, meat of white,
the graceful extensions of their necks.

How much of the world they had to shed
in just pushing themselves along.

How beneath the whiteness of their forms
such black legs churned.

Our children were trying to trick the geese
into eating ice cubes.

As the swans swam on,
serious, complete, of such a certain magnitude.

But their flaw was not their muteness.
Each wild length ended
in a clipped wing.

And how at night
they had to put themselves to sleep
behind that one clipped thing.

2. The Snow Geese

After the first snow
an edge comes on.
The dew that has gathered itself
all fall on the roof,
loosening itself from the eaves,
now stays, hard in the sun.
The roof is a sum
of its brilliant selves,
a white explosion of nerves.

North of the house
snow geese stand in a field,
silent, their acts pulled down,
their orange bills in the cold
announcing themselves.

Suddenly I'm up,
putting my hands on the pane,
wanting out with those geese.
My hands and wrists and arms
are fuses abroad with the cold.

And when the geese turn,
short bodies, their shadows firm
against the ground, I want to go forth
over and over again in the snow,
putting my flat hands down.

3. The Bull Elk

Even after he walked up to it,
crumpled on the ground,
there was a wrenched silence
to the place.

He bled the head downhill.
He cut along the belly line
from the brisket to the vent.
He went deeper through the muscles.

Pulling up, he used his fingers
as guides, slabbing himself
through the stiffening intentions
of its legs.

He avoided the intestines,
he went around the anus,
he split the pelvic bones.
Straddling back toward the head,

he used an axe to split
the chest, front to back,
then followed the gullet
and the windpipe to the tongue.

Cutting both, he pulled.
The heart and liver and lungs
and paunch came out.
The rumen he threw away,

what was left of the Trembling
Aspen and the Rose. He stepped
back from straddling the head.
He wiped his hands.

The tongue was simply thicker than
it had ever been.

4. The Eider

This is a different world, this St. Lawrence.
There is something older and thicker here.

Far out in this ocean of a river
the eider ducks, drifting in rafts, in sanctuaries,
are huge birds, stark white above
and black below.

Moniacs the Eskimos call them,
saying they line their nests with down,
working their bills as far
into their breasts as nature allows.

Not eating when they brood.

They say that when they come back from fielding
there is a long low croon of birds over the water,
in the dusk a line of beads
working its way back to the nest.

And then the brooding begins again,
and then the dark comes down.

5. The Hawk

Somewhere years from now
I hope I'm saying this
to my sons. Why the hawk
had hit the trap I couldn't guess.
In the face of it
it was pointless.

But it had hit the trigger
dead center with both feet,
for a moment lifting
that fatal weight
before the blind torque
of the trap had sprung.

After that its wings had clawed
at the sand for hours,
its cries had gradually sunk back
into its throat, although
its beak, thrust defiantly
at the stream, held on
to an animal yellow.

Then it had pulled everything in,
for a moment the hawk
and only the hawk's turn.
In that blind and beautiful light,
trying to hold on,
as the trap held on,
to what it was.

CARDINAL

A cardinal in the snow
is one of the few things
to recommend itself
without metaphor.

THE DOE

In the quarter light
of the morning
the doe slipped into
the clearing like brown smoke.

Above her
the outcropping of the rocks
held their breath,
her blood moved in her hams
like delicate water.

As she came down
through the draw
each of her steps
was a precise awakening
to an act undone.

The great bells
of her ears,
alive to sound,
hung there in time,

cast to announce
that single thing
out of tune
with the morning.

POET IN RESIDENCE AT A COUNTRY SCHOOL

The school greets me like a series
of sentence fragments sent out to recess.
Before I hit the front door
I'm into a game of baseball soccer.
My first kick's a foul; my second sails
over the heads of the outfielders;
rounding third base, I suck in my stomach
and dodge the throw of a small blue-eyed boy.
I enter the school, sucking apples of wind.

In the fifth-grade section of the room
I stand in the center of an old rug and ask,
where would you go where no one could find you,
a secret place where you'd be invisible
to everyone except yourselves;
what would you do there; what would you say?

I ask them to imagine they're there,
and writing a poem. As I walk around the room,
I look at the wrists of the kids,
green and alive, careful with silence.

They are writing themselves into fallen elms,
corners of barns, washouts, and alkali flats.
I watch until a tiny boy approaches,
who says he can't think of a place,
who wonders today, at least,
if he just couldn't sit on my lap.
Tomorrow, he says, he'll write.

And so the two of us sit under a clock,
beside a gaudy picture of a butterfly and
a sweet poem of Christina Rosetti's.
And in all that silence, neither of us can
imagine where he'd rather be.

SINGING A BIRD'S SONG

Begin.

Never ask where a call ends
and a song begins.

Before the sediment of the west
pulls down the sun,
sing until your feathers burn.

So you have only five notes:
try purity of tone.

Sing the weight the moment
of a single branch can hold.

THE RUNNER

He had been running a long time,
starting in the rain,
the sounds of his wet shoes
like shaken sacks of marbles
on the road.
And he had run into the sun,
he had run a long way into the sun,
until the sky came down
over his eyes, wet and heavy.
Somewhere in the ninth mile
he remarked how his lungs kept forcing
a muffled thunder from his mouth,
how the gravel in the sun
played out its hints of lightning,
how beside him his hands
pulled him along.
The right one shaped like
a hammer in a muscular red room,
going back to his father.
But as for taking matter
from his eyes, he let his left hand
do it. Or buttoning buttons
or directing sighs.
This is what he thought about,
entering the hills.
And going farther than
he had been in years,
he felt the cuts in the rocks
close about him,
felt the slim white blooms

of the milkweed combing the air.
And the valley where he worked
kept trailing off behind him,
slowly, systematically,
like some civilized fear.

HOW TO LIVE IN BUFFALO COUNTY

Bless the wind.

Listen to at least
three languages:
the county's, the township's,
your house.

Love distance like
a loon, read stones,
make wild flowers
familiar.

Live in this place,
hoping to get there.

FISHING, AT COOT SHALLOWS

Memory is a full pocket.
On slow fishing days
our hands go down
among the kisses and the scars,
among the rabbits' feet,
the things we've willed,
and we stand there,
having brought something up,
looking at ourselves.

MY MAD UNCLE'S MAD SONG FOR CHRISTMAS

One Christmas Eve, my mad uncle, a man-child injured
    at birth, took a large wooden bowl and walking through
    the gathering dark of the farmyard went down and put it
    on the low roof of the shed where we kept our guineas.
    He was very careful about it, and that night it snowed.
    I remember watching it through the bedroom window,
    falling softly, lighting up the garden.

The next morning I found my mad uncle in the kitchen.
    It was warm in there, and he was singing one of his
    mad songs while whipping milk and sugar and vanilla
    into the snow. And he kept on beating the beejesus out
    of the bowl until he stopped, and spooned snow ice
    cream into cereal bowls with blue barns on their bottoms.

Then he went out and put them down in the yard. What
    followed was the most absurd good love song of all,
    my mad uncle hovering over the bowls, singing down
    to the barn, telling the guineas and all of the rest
    of the faithful to come.

THE COYOTE

After I put the wounded coyote
in a box on the back porch
it crouched like a fawn hand
in a corrugated world.

It gave me more mistrust than
the box could hold,
and that night it howled,
its voice cutting through
the screen door and over
the fields.

And far in the hills
the voice, alone, materialized.

It kept climbing a rock.
All night it kept calling
something on the back porch
whose blood was feeding a box.

MILE RELAY, 4TH LEG

It's snowing,
the wind is bringing
millions of fragile runners
to their marks.

It's early spring, too early.

My sweat shirt
is tied around my neck
by the arms,
my sweat pants are hanging
in front of my legs
between me and the snow.

As I dance there,
waiting for the baton,
in the distance
the third legs of the relay
keep running.

Then everything stops.

It's 1950.

I'm standing waiting for a kid
whose name I've forgot.

THE SHOTGUN

I've always liked the way
the shotgun slid out of its case,
the barrel a long clean sound
against the zipper.
I remember I was ten
when I took it out for
the first time. It was heavy,
asking too much of my wrist.
And I remember telling my friends
what my father said about
its Damascus twist-steel barrels,
about having them tested
every so often for the latest loads.
That was years ago, years
since I tested my father.
Now as I wipe the gun oil
from the barrel, the blue-black metal
swims in the light like
a delicate snake.
What are old shoots but
moments of metal and feather?
Old hunts but times
we draw down on when we think
we have lost the edge?
Next fall when I walk
the uplands with the shotgun
cradled in my arms,
my academic sutures
will split open like
raw flowers in the fields.
And in the center of it all
there will be a hard silence
I will want to hold onto.

NEBRASKA

Going west when the sun is going down, following
the highways like light cords.

*

If Nebraska were the name of a Russian woman,
they could love her.

There would be a certain large-boned beauty
about her.

Or she would be dressed in black and lace.
Her waist would be small,
and she would drag her long dress over a floor into
a study lined with French books.

She would be a pawn in huge novels of war.

*

As it is, she is a woman of spare beauty.

*

Turning away from him so that the fine hollows of
her back were toward the bed,
she said, Why do you do this to me?

Why do you keep imagining me in other
places and states?

And why do you keep assuming our children
are unhappy?

From THE KEEPER OF MINIATURE DEER (1986)

OLD SUMMERS

This is a morning when the sky
comes down easily.
I remember my mother singing,
her rich contralto muted
just behind her lips,
her eyes in the kitchen busy
with her hands.
Even the painted tin
of the kitchen table, cold
as death, grew warm.

What she sang was a set piece
of the time, *White Ducks
on a Pond*. And when she came
to the line, *what little
sweet things do we remember
with tears*, her mouth opened,
filling the room
with a Wagnerian timbre.

It was a strange tone
to surround the small beets
and potatoes she was peeling,
but that was my mother,
as resonant as mornings
or old summers.

SMALLEST DAUGHTER

The way things go empty window by window.
Upstairs she changes herself. She draws herself
from her dress, letting her hair fall, turning
back to her bed. Then she steps from the window
into a different world. She moves into a sleep
so deep there is nothing to remember, nothing
at all. All night time swims in her room
like a swan. In silence now, smaller than
thought and softer now, close to dawn,
so close to birdsong.

COAT-OF-ARMS

Against a light blue sky
the family kite,
blood-red, among gulls.

DOWSER

He comes to the land
with nothing but a hazel stick
cut from a thicket,
and his hands.

From the place on the stick
where his hands go
he has cut the bark back,
and, green and willowy,

the stick is about to be
as current as a wish.
But there is nothing spectacular
about the man himself:

his overalls, stained cow dung
and the slop of years.
But what is his job if not to go down
through the sluff of generations

and to find, far from
the world's expectant mouths,
that character of that
most sacred stream?

For what is divination
but feeling brought to bear
upon the brightest of all
reckonings?

QUIXOTE'S MEDITATIONS ON A PLAIN

Things in the eyes
of some men
are never plain,
he said.

Nor are small figures
ever indicative
of their dreams.

Sancho,
were I to choose again
it would be a madness
more resonant than
it's ever been—

more ass for you,
more horse for me,
more wind.

THE KEEPER OF MINIATURE DEER

The keeper of miniature deer
was an old man with stiff knees.
He had the straight eyes of a child.
He walked the emperor's grounds,
speaking to the white swans
and the empress's pheasants.
In the compound of red deer,
among the musk and estrus,
he was especially fond of two old ones
born joined at the shoulders,
a stag with its rack huge and carbuncular
spreading out over a doe,
the old doe with eyes like fitful oil
over water. And he who knew nothing
of life after death, who lived
only to serve the miniature deer,
let them eat from his hands,
holding out salt in one,
in the other, grain,
softly calling their names,
saying *Mother* and *Father*.

THE CASTRATUS

> *—The Church's castration of gifted boy sopranos enabled them to sing on into manhood with the same high voices.*

Imagine one,
as if in an old painting,
standing to the back
and left of center.

Imagine how he feels
as the knives of light fall
through the cathedral windows,
his mouth open, formed
around the clear high note.

And then his going home,
the stunted green stairs
leading to his room,
his bed of quirk.

And imagine his saying
there is nothing he can do about it,
and floating his sweet silver voice
over the heads of Rome.

THE RIVER
—for Dutch Welch

Winter,
late afternoon,
the sun a pale flare
in the westering trees.

Here, the willows
have almost gone home
to the dark,
there is a perceptible
wind trailing the edges
of minutes.

This afternoon
it was warm.

And now my father,
picking up decoys, swings
lead weights around their necks,
his back to the west.

All day,
having moved in this river
like a pleasant doom,
his surgeries blending
with the buckbrush and trees,
he has had his eyes
unraveled by birds.

Tonight deer will unfold themselves
from the dark and come forth.

In the deepest channels
slush ice will form itself

in cold lacy jags,
the slews grow brittle
with ice.

I look west.

There is a single hole
in the clouds through which
time is escaping.

THE BREEDER OF ARCHANGELS (1991)

His name was Warloski. Anton Warloski. An old Bohemian who lived on the south side of town, across the tracks from the German bankers, he was someone I visited every Saturday morning as soon as my mother thought it was courteous. One winter I remember bicycling south, riding over railroad tracks which ran like long metallic icicles into the sun.

When I arrived, Warloski, his face frosted with stubble, was feeding his chickens. The chickens were in a run-down pen, behind dead-gray boards. They had bodies too small for their legs, and heads too big for their bodies. If Warloski were a breeder of chickens, something had gone radically wrong.

But I never said a word to him. After the first year he never gave me permission to go where he knew I was going. I just walked through the garden, which in the cold was like his chickens, stunted and gray of limb.

At the far end of his lot, so far south it was at the edge of the river, there was a small shed, its roof finished with tin, its door locked with a long piece of one-by-four. Which I turned like the minute hand of a clock and went in.

In time, Warloski came after me. There, on overturned buckets in a winter shed, our feet half-warmed by cobs, we watched the sun scatter itself through the cellophane windows. Around us on rich feet pranced Archangels, pigeons crowned and bronzed with a celestial sheen. An old country breed, they had been brought over by his father from Slovakia, but the originals were dull, like oil on water on a cloudy day.

Warloski said he wanted more, wanted their feathers to speak a fire the way the painting did in St. Theresa's rectory, when Stepanka had the windows clean. The light came in and swam across its bronze. He said he'd seen it also in a wind storm when the wires came down. Black crackled, and there were shades to its nerves. Strange greens and oranges and purples! He said if someone could breed that way the sun could paint divinely.

Then he stopped. Picking an Archangel from the floor, he cupped its iridescence in his hands, and with a finger as thick as my wrist he began to stroke the bird's breast. Then, as if confessing to God, he said, *You see, a certain sheen has escaped me.*

I looked hard. As a kid all I could see was a bronze bird set on fire by the sun. Warloski got up. Then looking down, he changed my life with with his wine-stained mouth. He said *Yes, you can take some home.*

From THE PLATTE RIVER (1992)

NOW, AT THE EDGE OF THIS RIVER

Wade in. The river which grips
your ankles is the smoothest chain.
Even, still, it has you.

What it asks is the initiation
of your skin, your feet
given over to drift sand.

Look: ahead a long sandbar
has risen like an ancient whale,
head down, its flukes thrust into land.

If you want to know its graver self,
walk carefully its taut arch,
then take its lead.

Step off again.
In the shallows you'll find grains
of sand which flake like gold.

Be glad for motes. But go on,
go much darker, dive in.
The water wants only to involve you.

WHITE CRANES IN SPRING

—for Marcia

There were white cranes that spring,
the feathered bowls of their wings
scooping out air, lifting them up
like unstemmed peonies.

Over the Gulf they could only circle
so long as Galveston's halos
before they broke for the Platte,
a blue braid which runs through Nebraska.

For centuries they had danced on
corn bones, on the fossilized memories
of nomads, or played contrabassoon
to the winter through the long folds

in their syrinx. In each bird
was a red germ, the unison cipher
of sex. And that spring,
paired up, we too flew north,

following the kissed-out leaves
of the willows, as if for a million springs
we had said the same thing
and were crying it hoarsely.

THE PAINTER AND THE RIVER

He wants to be there at dawn
to paint the vermilion channels
and the sun's gong. Or there
when the river turns silver,

making it lithe; when noon fattens it,
reddens it. If he can only cup
water in his palm, in one quick stroke
dipping up the mother-stock,

he can paint the trees
like Chinese written characters,
each one styled by weather
and wood love; or capture

the water as an utter of sunlight,
a trickle of balm, where
the late afternoon river is golden,
like the odor of quince and lemon.

And he wants to return in winter,
feeling those great sheets of ice
building up, slugging down,
grinding the edges of the sandbars,

macerating the roots of the willows.
He wants to stand on that ice,
on that blue-white time, looking down.
And he wants to be there at night,

when black, the river flows
like a woman in a silk sheath,
when it loses its smooth gray tones
and takes on the moon.

THE VET

He came home from Vietnam stunned into silence.
Bodies kept exploding in his head, and he built
a cabin on accretion land owned by his father.
In time the river worked on him, the river
and a crippled sandhill crane, and a labrador,
yellow. The gate to his place was plastered
with red signs: **KEEP OUT**, they said.

I remember him in class. Once he stopped
to talk about what Robert Frost had said
about going back into the land.
Never confuse retreat with escape, Frost said.
Now he sometimes sends me notes from the river.
It looks as if the light is good again.

THE RIVER AS A FIGURE OF LOVE

The sand bar was the perfect page.
Our steps had written themselves
precisely across it, and the bar itself
was a small island which spoke
elevated truths.

Give me your hand, you said.
Water's skin is so unbelievably supple
it is easy to step into its life.

Without it, the air would know only
spiritual nuptials; the earth
only general truths. And the atoms
of the sun would split themselves
in their own parched throats.

It was moonless. The river
flowed in a dextrous silence.

Those who cannot love
have never been inside it.

TELL YOURSELF

—for Larry Holland

Tell yourself one must have a love for ducks
to wade a braided river in the late October sun,

someone who has learned to dead-man stock tanks,
rip-rap towheads, walk thin ice.

Imagine him saying shovelers and mergansers,
goldeneyes and scaup, and mallards

with green-heads like God's celestial whole notes
falling from the heavens.

Someone like this must love the dark, the kind
of strong black night before the sun comes up

that makes him trust the compass in his brain stem;
someone who in following his father,

a lifeline of advice thrown over
the old man's shoulder,

knows the ways of dark water
and how a blind is found.

THE SMALL RELIQUARY

On sand, in a shriveled-up stream bed,
a small reliquary of deer bones burns in the sun.
Touch them: a bleached leg going nowhere,
the eyeholes of a skull caught in a stare.

And there, among the tiniest runes,
the scapular of a fawn needs you to help it
remember. Hold aloft a tooth fallen
from its jawbone. Help it try to gnaw air.

And among these bones, two empty shells:
one Federal, one Winchester: one blue,
one red, both double-ought buck.
Notice how their plastic blooms in the sun.

Once both spoke, racketing the landscape
and spreading out a pattern of death.
Now they lie mute on the lips of the drift sand,
uncrimped, brass-rusted, choked by the wind.

RIVER DEER

Near a bridge south of Wood River, Nebraska,
two deer have slid out of the willows
and are wearing bare air.

They are standing mid-stream,
their ears great racquets.

Just beyond them
a deep-running channel is a long musical rope
tying itself in soft knots.

The deer look up at me high on the bridge.
Our eyes are beads of the moment.

AFTER A BLIZZARD

This morning there is a center to silence,
a snow no one has walked upon,

and the wind has folded up like a mastiff
deep in sleep.

In this world a fox has stopped walking,
for a moment neither going on

nor doubling back, but standing stock-still
in the indicative mood.

What it sniffs is a seamless air.
What it wears is a white wedge of head.

Somewhere generals and politicians are clanging
like brass in their haste.

And there are pedants with passive voices
losing themselves in a blur of intentions

while remaining strong in their rank.
But here there is nothing to forgive,

nothing at all, as if white
were the presence of absence. . . .

TWO SNAILS

Just beyond the pond scum this morning
I looked down into a pool of two snails.

Two brown pebbles,
coils on muscular feet.

Then they began moving toward one another.
The distance was vast.

Whole civilizations of algae were transforming
themselves, while rootless, others were perishing.

But over and over, their shy selves gliding out,
the snails kept bringing

the huge burden of their lives
up to their feet.

As if each foot were a tongue,
as if each carried a chrysalis of syllables.

And when they coupled, lines came together
in a slow commotion of slugs.

Small, they were the knit
of a parable.

THE TALE OF WATER

There is a moment
when the eyes of water
grow violet,

when like amethysts,
blue diamonds,
they see from a summit,

and the air is full of alarm—
something has happened
to water,

it has been caught in an ache,
frozen in angles,
spiculed.

On the edge of the mountains,
in towering falls,
there are long frozen tongues.

In nuclear winter
how long would the leaves be green
in your memory?

Even the weed sings,
wearing clear pearls,
orbed in original energy.

This is the tale of water.
Listen hard.

From THE MARGINALIST (1992)

THE MARGINALIST

Before him are long tall margins of vellum
and on the page the characters sacredly drawn.
His pens sleep. Beside them the onyx eye
of the ink. And he looks at the table.

Then opening small vessels of folium,
of indigo and orpiment, white and red lead,
he offers his hands. The kermes, or carmine red,
weeps with Christ's blood, remembering.

And the ultramarine, elaborately prepared
by the Arabs and as precious as gold,
rests in its silver cask, on which are
peacock heads with eyes of lapis lazuli.

A door creaks. Brother Jasper slips out
for another night of the flesh. Down the hall
the old abbot himself falls dangerously into
his sleep, the other cells collapsing in darkness.

But in the marginalist's, verdigris is opened,
the extract of malachite. Outside, where
the dark muscles its way toward the coast
or plays the empty eyeholes of a Viking's mask,

there is dead weight. But inside there's oil light,
and a slim green line that begins its pilgrimage
across a maiden page.

NOUNS

On a stairway leading to a space
beyond which there are no steps
there is a small wind made up
of the cries of the dead.

These are our others,
the most recent breaths of
who we were.

Yet there are days
when we are more than alive
because of our stories,
when in that great humpbacked muscle
in our mouths there is sound
and its way is long.

Nouns: any of a class
of words designating small births
and later discoveries.

THE UNICORN

This is the shape the horse has always wanted,
free, harnessed only to myth, ridden hard
by the speculative head.

When a unicorn steps out of a horse's hooves,
it casts no shadow.

In the moonlight it is inexhaustible.
No one can run it to death.

*

For a time whatever it is moves in the wind.

The breeze has a certain flex to it,
the sky is ignited by stars.

The eyes of the unicorn are blue, circled with silver.

*

In possibility the image is always the answer.

To carry them into different countries
they were given imaginary beasts.
Some wanted to go fierce, some gentle.

Their clothes and other effects were burned.
They were put naked on unicorns.

*

Sometimes the price we pay for belief
is a thin silver coin resembling

the moon in the morning.

Its edge is soft, yet sharp,
it has an invisible center.

We enter by taking one step,
without preparing our faces.

*

Having come a long way,
no longer riding on the original beast,
some of them had a strip of back, a piece of flank,
a section of horn.

They handled them longingly.

Some of them even cried as if
they knew what it was.

SAPPHIRE

1.

At the bottom of sight,
beyond the clear corundum,
there are deep blue needles
with the weight of light.

2.

There is a true story
of a small sun room
where eyes, a stone,
and love were one.

3.

A sapphire is no petal.
It is a crystalline nut,
a fruit, a wish settled.

We wonder why we haven't
come to it before.

4.

The stone that worked miracles
was worn so casually
from town to town, bowing
to the sauerkraut and broccoli,
listening to the most innocuous talk.

5.

The way blue changes,
and in change is true.

There are so many places
we would like to spend the light.

6.

This is the hard grace of our
lives, this is what we keep,
this is what we've earned to.

7.

Sapphire,
that clear blue silence
after the guests have left.

HOME FROM THE WORD STORE

Sometimes walking home from the university
I think of all the effort
that goes into extruding bushes
of words at the place where I work,

and of people like me
walking along at the end of the day,
tired of tending plants
in their mouths (a ridiculous

figure); who nonetheless
want them cut out, but instead
are walking quite casually,
one foot at a time,

dropping limb after limb.
And before us are those great
slabs of concrete like oceans
rolling us home.

How we hate sparrows,
those chattering prefixes
of speed. And the weight
of Mercedes. So we dream,

of those un-Yeatsian rag shops
dear to our hearts—
old overalls, smocks,
unvarnished shoe-trees.

Yet not even these hurry us along.
We step slowly from curbs,
as tired as the world's loose familiars,
rusted metals, old nouns.

FIRST BOOK APOCRYPHA

Eve, contrary to all reports,
I made you first.

Before one word had closed,
you were the germ in my broad urge,
the love that quickened me to form.

Shall I tell you how it was before you were?
Black snowflakes fell.
Darkness was my only circumstance.

And after this dark had bruised my head,
I saw you coming toward me,
holding my diminished love in your light hands.

OLD WOMAN

In a hospital bed an old woman
  lies sleeping, her mouth
    open, her jaws

unhinged. She has no muscle tone,
  there is a pleating
    of her skin,

what few teeth she's left ground down.
  But with codeine's help,
    and in a balloon

of sour breath, she dreams.
  A young doctor has
    taken her hand,

and a hundred of estrogen's birds
  are again leaving
    her dovecote.

White, more sexual than angels,
  they circle her room.
    And as age

begins to slip from her shoulders
  like the sheerest of things,
    she dreams:

of a sexuality white in intent,
  of a body pure and
    un-schemed.

LOT'S WIFE

Someone else turned back,
or how were we to know
the magic of her olive skin
seared white, burned crystalline?

And for how many centuries
did an unrelenting god
perpetuate her as a sharp
memory of himself?

If so, of what is she
a definition really?
A pillar of undulance
gone astray? Of curiosity

standing corrected?
And on those mornings
when a single drop of dew
forms in her eye,

she weeps for whom?
For someone too hard
to temper his justice
with a newer love?

Is this what she's
a testament of?
Is this her longer lot?
Why then do we imagine

she's more than an escarpment
of a woman, that the wind
on her fractured lips
is still her own?

And that each small breath
she utters from her crust
is a lithe remembrance of
a loveliness she once owned?

THE CHRISTMAS WREATHER

Scheduled for weeks, she showed up one morning
at breakfast, her basket layered with grasses
and the scraps of old clothes; and eyeing us
still in our pajamas and robes, she quickly

turned to her work, clearing the dining room table,
skootching her ample posterior into one
of our cane-seated, ladder-backed chairs.
Her reflection in the top of the table looked

like a pock-marked moon, but oh, could she weave.
Into long grama grasses went the pulse
of red ginghams. And it was then that we discovered
where the centers of the best eyes had gone.
They had gathered in hers.

Round and round went her hands in
an ever-returning song, weaving a cyclic magic
into our linear lives. With her fingers
she knitted up space, tucking time in.
Just as casually she rhymed cloth and stems.

Later, in her room across town, she felt her hands
rouse in themselves and her dream deepening.
The edges of time had come loose, and she was
weaving into them shadows and the threads
of the sun,

while God, like some rich woman standing behind
her, stood stunned.

OLD GERMAN WOMAN

What she was, she was.
When she appeared,
she appeared to be.

Not having to suffer
herself into being,
she simply yearned,
having the ground
sense necessary.

But when she moved,
she created a field,
and when she loved,
it was like water
building up inside
its own bead.

For a long time,
flying abroad, she
was a small hedge bird
rising and falling.

Until hanging on
like the slenderest nerve,
in the exhausted fields,
under the low bush
of evening, she became
a slight tone.

And when she paused,
it mattered deeply.

MY DEAR MISS DICKINSON,

I regret to say, my brother,
Gerard Manley Hopkins,
now in the north of Wales,
is terribly ill. Could he,
he would thank you for your poems,
especially the one which begins,
"I cannot want it more—
I cannot want it less—
My Human Nature's fullest force
Expends itself on this."

Young, in choice-limbo,
Gerard often sat at our kitchen table
with his cursed/blessed words,
in love with the oddest shapes.
But I dare say
the right one found,
he carried it home the way
a Northumbrian would bring
a lost sheep into the kitchen,
his arms and shoulders dead,
his spirit almost broken.

Miss Dickinson, I do not
fully understand my brother
or his poems, but I know this.
The right one made,
he walks in peace, wearing
its corona; and how long
or brief it lasts is not
the substantial question.

And so I thank you for Gerard,
whose words right now

play across his body weakly.
Next to the Father, though,
silence has always been
the best ghost for my brother.
It also makes demands.
In time he may be strong
enough to write again,
he may be fit. If not,
his life for it.

>   Gerard Manley Hopkins'
>   younger sister.

Winter, 1874.
>   In the reign of Christ Our Lord
>   and the Queen, Victoria.

From CARVED BY OBADIAH VERITY
   (1993)

CARVED BY OBADIAH VERITY

Once, when I was looking at some decoys carved
a hundred years ago,
curlews and plovers, ruddy turnstones,
I thought of how they began,
as stutters in wood, gouges and flutes,
skewers and judgments of beauty.

They were simple things.
In their heartwoods the grains ran on,
the primitive music of fibers.
And as I stood there, I began to imagine
Verity working, the acts of his hands,
the pauses, in which he kept

mounting something finer than skin
on those things. And what came over
the years was more than a touchable
silence. There was something
in those shore birds I was supposed
to pass on, from Verity,

like the deep intelligence of love,
and I left that place full of
breed, and brood, and cross-hatching.

THE GLASSED BIRD

Stuck in dry ice
the crystal bird was a mask.
Even its eyelids,
forever frozen in sight,
had been caught in
a beautiful moment.

It was a remarkable feat,
the emperor's artisans
capturing a wild bird
in glass, without burning
its rare iridescence.
The emperor himself was dead.

Before his artisans could
finish their task
he slept underground
with a thousand clay warriors
cast in funereal gloom,
his eyes darkly pitched.

While every morning
outside his old windows
the day slowly warmed;
and a bird of free beauty,
perched in red bud,
turned liquid with song.

FIVE IRISH PICTURES

1. The Glassworker

For forty years in such burned hands
the passionate quarrel: the way
his rigor held, then softened,
spun into iridescences by line,
tone, the elements of love.

But near death, when the hard
expression of himself in glass
was not enough, he cradled
the whiskey in his massive hands,
saying, I want purer.

Something like a last blown breath
absent of regret would do, he said.
Or a simple taking-off in which
my own small pulse might become
the last circumference of myself.

I know I'm good, he said,
but let's say in that moment
between my death and fame
there might be something light-caught,
pure, undreamed—even
crystalline with good oblivion . . .

then, aware of the absurdity,
he laughed.

2. Barley Cove, West Cork

Across the blue-black water
something like a dozen swans.
How can they be so calm?
Ignorance is white feathers.

As time ripples from them
we never see their black legs
churn, nor the faint red sparks
which snap and lapse

between their nerves. We lack
the innocence to call them on.
In the rushes, old greens run.
Over the hills bigots suck

marrow from each other's bones.
Even the lass down by the water,
with the parts we used to die for,
turns.

3. Old Men, Aran Islands

None of them chose their stone houses.
Their houses chose them, rocks lifted
one by one, fitted together in design,
flint edges kissing each other

in prehistoric recognition. And outside,
wherever one looks, paved distance
slates the eye. Inside, an inward breed
of men still sit at tables,

the air between their fingers dark
and heavy, stones vaulting their lives.
Once the sons of women now long gone,
in churchyards they have bitten

their mothers' names from stone.
And from time to time, going down
through the rundales of the walls,
they have stopped among the gravestones,

opening the strongholds of their hands.
There they have touched words into a smoothness,
words like *Angela* and *Anne.*

4. Stone Rubbing, Dowth Passage Grave

Slowly my lead begins,
falling like gray rain across
an ancient rose,
then moving up,
its slate inscription climbing
as my pencil climbs.

But this grave slab's squat,
squared by a hand,
its fingers blunt,
its cramped flesh thickened
by the chiseling hours.

Was he hunched by trade,
ragged of youth?
Was he, too, measured
by the rain's soft teeth?

On this stone
old evidence of art,
a primitive rose,
the hard unfolding of
a neolithic dream . . .

and my rubbing mocks his work.

In this churchyard filled
with shadows etched
with sound
the white shoes of the tourists
simply glare and bloom.

5. The White Deer of Mallow

Then there was one stag running,
the soft Irish air on its shoulders,
its great lungs red with memory's blood,
and I remembered what I was told as a child,

how the lives of some things went out
to the edge of the world, to places
where ghosts filtered from the mists,
great pagan movings with their ears flared,

their pale heads cocked. And these wraiths,
feeling running things fist and relax,
fist and relax, had wind again in their faces,
the trees leaning in. Until a jerk or start

would fall over this bone-hoard.
And there at the edge of the world,
remembering hard in the plenty of time,
they would suddenly find themselves running,

the red seal and signature again in their eyes.

From THE WORDS WHICH MARRY ME TO YOU (1995)

    1.

What is it that speaks
before a word is spoken

if not the compatible ghosts
who glide between us in this house?

In the light where two circles meet
we can see the respect

they have for each other.
For theirs is not only

a marriage of unspoken vowels,
it is a consonance of silence.

And over the years we too
have come to feel what they know:

in love's white ovals
there are perpetual hellos.

    6.

However dark the night,
love makes it less opaque.

A lilac will leave a thrush
in heart-shaped song,

and long after dark the thrush's afternotes
will gleam on every leaf's dark tongue.

It is not an illusion of the moon:
when I am gone,

these words which marry me to you
will be that thrush's song.

From FIRE'S TONGUE IN THE CANDLE'S END (1996)

LETTER TO MY CHILDREN

What more can I say
about that day when the wind
stops moving me with its invisible hands,
and birds fly so far into the distance they
never come back;

when the river dries up,
sanding my nouns,
and time stops kneading
its small miraculous clusters;

that day when I'll no longer
look hard for the us
in myself, wrestling poems
on the mat of my tongue;

in short, when I begin
to unshape what was born,
and the light is someone else's
to play with?

OF NOTE TO A YOUNG WRITER

—while looking over her shoulder

If you're one of those
for whom the best sounds
are like conch shells
held to your ear,
swirl out of yourself
the hard whorl of words.

And think of it this way,
your journey over,
your poem's just begun,
listen to what laps out of silence
and comes ashore at the edge
of the word.

TO A FRIEND STARTING A NEW POETRY JOURNAL

Really, why build a martin house today?
Even if you dream it over a cup
of coffee in the kitchen, why not say
sparrows will get it anyway. And up,

just the idea of going up, will disturb the lie,
the smooth brown lie of coffee in your hand.
So why not settle back in raw self-mockery
and undercut your absurd pro-bird stand?

Oh, I grant you, if you go fictionally so well
you undo morning till it lies like lumber,
why then I'd pick a board and cut the holes
with such belief they'd martin out all sparrows.

And once in, I'd try for greater grace.
I'd go more purple than a martin purpling space.

LETTER TO PETER

Peter, for an hour this afternoon I'll go
sports illustrated, waiting for my doctor
who says that time in a waiting room may be iodine
on a raw psyche, but what are we going to do.

You remember, him, don't you,
the guy who was shot with the tenpenny nail
two years ago when they remodeled his office?
The worker with the nail gun thought

he had a solid wall. What he had was
an old doorway which led to Pack's pancreas.
So for a week his fingers never spoke,
and his voice lay in drifts behind his teeth.

Which is not unusual, at least that part
about his voice. You remember how inaudibly
Pack talked? Well, he still does.
When he speaks to bedpans, electric scalpels,

and those fates he calls his nurses,
the whole clinic asks, "Uh Eh Where Doctor?"
and 15 years of these requests wind the place
like gauze. But it's his two-dimensional life

which irritates me. His hands are a teutonic
blitz, but his mouth lumbers like an axle.
Today, just before I put the madonna spirit
of my inner arms on that cold examining table,

just before he checks the tonsils of my prostate,
I'm going to amaze him with *my* carpentry.
I'm going to show him how the oak of English syntax
slides off the edges of my tongue,

show him how a totem tune lies fetally in words,
how it contains a pulse which goes back beyond
the pancreas, back to the smithcraft of a racial gland
which proves it's there by outliving us

as we live out ourselves. Peter, I'll show him
how the un-ethered mouth's a probe.
And you know what? He won't buy it.
He'll let my blood speak simply into gauges,

let my heart talk crests and troughs of EKG,
let my urine say whatever it says residually.
Then, led by his hands, he'll go next door
to visit Agnes James. I wonder, Peter,

when she feels his sterile blitz,
will she be sore amazed?

TO A BEGINNING POET

1. Words like water,
like drops of sound,
each with an intent
so clear it can be
seen through—
go ahead, try one
on your tongue.
What is it if not
a small bulb
in an enormous room?

And if you're ready,
write it down.
Notice how it travels
back in time,
a kin to one
once scratched in stone,
or another drawn
from the flute end
of a quill.

Slow down.
Or impetuous,
dive in.
Words are
hummingbirds
with trips
as long as history.

2. In our century
the greatest victory
of the sadists
is not our deaths.
It is our lives-

in-death.

Having made it
laughable to leach
music from the wind,
the nihilists have won.

Still, in a single bulb
in Auschwitz
there burns a filament
so absurd it cannot be
explained. This
is the great mystery
at the heart of.

3. Take the light out
of your words
and watch how dark
your eyes become.

And keep writing
down, work hard
on your grains.

Whoever you are
lives under
countless laminations.

4. Because money is wealth,
and wealth rarely poetry,
most of the world
will think you odd.

If you were to tell them how
silence is a god

with many eyes,
and how you turned

toward him, one boy,
of many; and how you
learned that absence is
a river, not a scar,

a current of such delicate
fires it bears all the names
of violet, would they
be silent?

No, that is not their way.
Most men define themselves
with vague and periodic cries,
and that someone calm

could be so active
in a war for independence
would confuse them.
You would not even be

an idle in their eyes.

5. Go out, never write
in a glass house.
The least spirit dies
for the want of matter.

Essence is no substitute
for the lowliest flower,
and your words can never
say what stones say,
but they can try.
In coming closer to what

a stone says, language loses
many of its lies.

6. To play a small candle on
a moonless night,
a voice of light
among the politics of black;

to be the instrument
of what wants to sing
and un-attracted
to debris and ruin;

to stand up for something
falling down the page,
the significance
of the brief poetic moment—

how does this differ
from those
dressed to kill
in fashionable cliches,

except to say what
they can never say,
to let the heart
of language have its way,

fire's tongue
in the candle's end,
of what you've loved,
and how you've been.

ABOUT YOUR CLASSROOMS

—for Laura Rotunno

The unimaginative believe there are no rooms
which remember those who absent them,

that absence vacuums everything
in its sleep.

Not so. For years what moves
in a classroom are its vital ghosts.

Oh, it's true, those who hated these rooms
or suffered them impassively are gone.

But not you. The good memory of yourself
is what you've earned to.

For you these classrooms have been
like the ivory of a narwhal's tusk,

and you our scrimshaw artist
intricate at work.

You have honored us
by taking such remarkable care.

Few shape absence into memorable air.

SOME WORDS FOR MY SON, A NOVICE HUNTER

Every pickup has its own music,
its bumps and squeaks.
These are the plain songs
it sings to hunters.

Each plum thicket is a knot,
an organic knit. Only
in youth is it pheasanted
or nothing.
If you shoot a quail before
you're 20, thank your luck.

Between 20 and 40, say you're good.
After that, shoot off your mouth,

tell old stories, use quick verbs.
And learn to hunt the hunt,
rather search than shoot.
In some far field

you may find yourself.
Be blessed with a wood duck's
plumage. Startled by it,
be tongue-tied by its beauty.

But try to speak of it just
before your death.
It will add rare colors
to your life.

TO VERN, ABOUT A FLANKER

Breaking from the huddle,
he begs a portrait
no camera can give him,

of his father running all day,
of his mother catching eggs
thrown from the lofts of barns.

In the howling bowl of a Saturday afternoon,
he watches a cornerback wave
his forearm clubs,

and then he's gone,
beyond the free safety,
measuring a liquid distance of yard-lines,

picking seams in the sunlight.
Because this is the way he is,
always was,

stretched out,
his toes just kissing the turf,
a palm at the end of a crowd.

TO A NUDE SUNBATHER

Now you walk naked in the sun,
swan-boned, the obverse
of the sniggering grin.

And light loves you,
enters every pore; to bloom
upon your breasts and thighs.

You were before the sword,
antecedent even to the word,
the air honoring you

with tender habits only skin
can wear. A sleeve of breeze.
Wind's skirt between your thighs.

And our anthologies?
Poets still fumble with your breasts,
your nakedness our index, and their test.

THE UNDERTONES

—for Gen Welch, 1905-1993

In that small room where
you played the piano,
you tried to teach me how
to feel the inside of a note,

how all along its inner arc
there was a womb of sound.
Listen, you said, and sang
a tone so light with dark

it held onto itself longer
than any note I'd heard.
Today, I listen hard.
If memory is a fetal dark,

then all along the inside
of your longest pause
you are your own rich echo.
And I'm no longer young,

no longer ear-dead
to the undertones of love.

THERE IS NO WIND IN HEAVEN

There is no wind in heaven. Every leaf,
like every soul, never touches another.
Each greens in its own resplendence.

And there are no dead branches in heaven
combing the air, no moans in the eaves,
no whistling nor-westers in gold gutters.

God, how I'll miss the wind wherever
I am. I think the dead might like
a breath of it on the edge

of their porcelain souls;
or its strong palm slapped broadly
against their rich complexions.

Children love the wind. In the winter
they bundle up to let it in.
There must be someplace for the dead

where children's voices color every
extremity of winter, where their vigor
makes mortal every branch, however bare.

I've always thought the wind is the sky
come down, but there is no sky in heaven.

From A BRIEF HISTORY OF FEATHERS (1996)

BALTIMORE ORIOLE

This morning the oriole
is a good carpenter,
working itself
for the sake of its nest.

Hounding the right bits of grass,
it has turned flight
into a muscular blossoming.

The air is something
it keeps slipping into;
it is what it beats
into breath with its life.

Tonight the sky will be hung
with migrational stars;
it will be the dark hunting
grounds of owls, the briefer tomb
of anything sleeping.

But tomorrow the oriole
will be at its work again,
and it will be singing.

BARN OWL

High in the rafters of the barn,
against the opening where
the ropeless pulley hung,
something the bird people call
Tyto alba, and what we felt
was the Mother of the White Mask,
suddenly set sail.

There was no sound, only
its onyx eyes, the rich tones
of its back and chocolate skull cap,
and of course that face of white.

And in that moment when we lost
our sight, that is, when our eyes
went out of us, following that bird
as if it were a long soft nerve
into the evening, no one,
no one stirred.

And through the hayloft door
we heard our mother's voice
calling us from the back steps
of the house, as if that owl could speak,
as if in our childlike world,
something beyond the dark,
deep, deep into the night,
could call us in to sleep.

THE BROWN GROUSE

A softness falls over the ground.
North of the barn the brown grouse
are turning into winter, every other
brown feather saying they are summer birds
slipping out of themselves, leaving
the bittersweet's berries. Neither
senses the thin whine in the few
remaining leaves of late November.
The female is whiter. The male's eyes
have turned rich and carnelian.
The winter is drawing them on,
white is coming out of their blood's
root. Now they are walking away
from the house on feathered feet,
they are walking out of themselves
into the cold ripe fields of winter.
In a softness such as this the unicorn
was born, with its eyes of palatable onyx.

THE MUTE SWANS

One by one a hundred mute swans
were snowing the lake with silence.

TURKEY VULTURE

Ugly, it looks like bad prose,
and flies as if the whole world
were made of ball-bearings.

THE DEAD KINGBIRD

—in memory of Bill Stafford

Long ago I picked up
a flower with wings
and carried it home.

A breath of decay
was slowly circling
its body,

death was
a figurative bird
taking off.

But there in the dark
of my youth that kingbird
mounted itself.

There in that place
from which all surrenders come
it began singing

a singular love,
one wing a small parenthesis,
the other more than an end to it,

and each generation
has left it dead
and renewed.

BLACK TERN

Black tern over the slough,
the grass bending in the wind,
the light a pale gold dust
upon the water.

Where is she now, the one
who knew the quick silence
of my life, who turned
when I turned?

So light she could tease
ascendancy from the slightest wind,
strong enough to throw herself
at storms which might un-bone her.

Now the wind blows, the grass
waves, the light spatters itself
upon the dark blue waters.

THE LAST WILD PASSENGER PIGEON

Only now that it is gone
does it appear to have come
from a strange country.

Once, in preening the feathers
on its back, its bill kept
tailing off into a deft blue world

only to return; its iridescence
was composed of small electrical storms,
its breast softer than doe's skin.

But when it fell into history,
little planets of grapeshot—
nuts and bolts and nails—

fired out of a ten-gauge
sailed on over somebody's field.
Otherwise when it fell,

there was only a small buff sound,
and that long slim form
it had always believed in.

POSTCARD ABOUT A FALCON

Like a ripped silence
it fell with the speed
of black enamel.

And hit,
my best pigeon flew apart
like a tea rose shaken
in a child's fist.

Summer was snowing.

OSTRICH

Most of the time it is content
to be what it is, passing its days
by pointing its long slim neck
toward indeterminate meaning.

Grotesque, almost having no head,
it walks partially naked through the world.
For it, flight is a truncated memory.
Still, there are times when it remembers

what it was supposed to be,
a small bird with a silver head
and a human face,
nesting in an immortal tree.

THE CRANES

—for Stan Smith

As I lay in bed this morning,
the window open, the cranes going north,
in a half sleep I thought
this is what it's like
after hours into a migratory flight,
the landscape so far away it's lost,
my limbs and muscles separated
from my head, consciousness
turned in upon itself.

Somewhere above me the cranes
with their slow stiff wings
had pulled out of the river.
After veering toward the sandpits
to avoid the cottonwoods,
rising over the highways,
over the wetlands and stubble,
they had ordered themselves in loose V's
above Kearney.

Over the courthouse the lead males
were letting out their long-fluted voices,
falling around the head of the buffalo
on the county building. Then
over town, past the big lightless bulb
of the water tower, and north,
all the time gathering height to join
the geese that had been on the wing
for at least 12 hours, their limbs
and muscles as slow and as regular
as heart-beats, their eyes seeing
but not seeing, the worlds inside their heads

full of the distance we call dreams.

Somehow I remember all of this
this morning. The woman coming in
through the window had the hands
of spring.

TO A SPARROW HAWK

I saw you in the sour gray light
of the freeway's exhaust,

hanging in the air from habit,
the white feathers of your underwings

fiercely angelic,
your yellow eye cocked to one side.

I was far from the plains,
and you had come.

I was sick with the metallic stench of cars,
and you had dropped down,

hunting the grooves in the asphalt,
the rubber's dumb runs.

In their cars men and women were fleeing
the city. Deep in their lives

faults had opened up,
and they were praying

to a small hawk to take them,
to take them beyond the cement's ash pit

where money breeds with its green flagellations
and its formal sexual cries.

SCENE I, INVOLVING YOU AND AN OWL

If you cannot return to a scene like this,
in time you will,
a bedroom with its old plaster walls,
the moon soft in the garden,
and beyond the garden a line of mulberry trees.
Just below the window
there will moonflowers, open, calm,
in their foliate moments.

But whatever it is,
it will invite you, sit with you,
taking you back,
until something, perhaps an owl sets sail,
coming carefully over the garden.

And there will be
nothing gauzy, sentimental about it,
because just before the glass it will flare,
opening its wings four times their ordinary size,
like a huge pale fire upon dark waters.

And in that room you will become a child,
something lighter than the shadow of an owl
passing over you, creating a shiver in your skin,
an orphaned nerve, making the window,
an ordinary thing, deeply foreign.

From EVERY MOUTH OF AUTUMN SAYS GOODBYE (1996)

After 20 years as a poet-in-residence
the university gave me
the perfect retirement gift,
an ornamental pencil with no lead.

*

In our run-on lives
a poem is a vertical moment.

*

The honest use of language is the ultimate political act.

*

Few good poems are fastballs.
Most are curves and sliders.

*

Write much. Publish little.

*

Once into a poem, write for its life.

*

The long shelf of poetry will tell you
baubles are not the soul's merchandise.

*

Make your words strong enough
to take and give blows.

*

Writing about things real,
we're sometimes fortunate enough
to make them beautiful too.

*

No really good poem goes along
with the official version of life.

*

As for students, most of them
think poetry is an intestinal stage
they're passing through.

*

Write down.
Work hard on your grains.
Whoever you are lives under countless laminations.

*

The easy is what we dream of.
The hard is what defines us.

*

Because the real always defeats the ideal,
it is wiser to have a good heart than a big head.

*

Anyone who writes poetry runs the risk of
being a wordwit, a wordbag, a warbler.

*

Every would-be writer has one good poem
in his hidden head.

*

Certain words are always looking for poets
to do them justice.

*

Value silence.
Be wise enough to let it have its say.

*

Work your talent. Work the hell out of it.

*

Listen hard.
Listen so hard you can hear whispers
at the ends of your breaths.

*

In writing, never know where you're going.
Just honestly try to get there.

*

An epitaph for a poet's tombstone:

*He tried to keep
both eyes open.*

*

When you read, check your ideologies at the door. Let
the poem be a room which brings you
to your senses.

*

Always leave your children a few poems to grow up to.

*

Haiku are one-fingered waves.

*

Read well to read even better.

*

Have you ever noticed that even our worst poems sing
on their way to the dump?

*

Our hope? To write one poem
with a truly remarkable shelf life.

*

She said, "Dr. Blank, you say nothing well."
Thanking her for the compliment, he offered to walk
her to her car.

*

Write because you have to.
In the long run all other reasons don't amount to much.

*

Nothing beats walking home
with a small accomplishment lengthening your bones.

*

Everyone stands by words.
Which are your companions?

CRANES: A BOOK OF HOURS (1996)

with Gene Fendt

MATINS

Mid-river, dark sleep
of birds, calm hunch and fold
of psalm and bone.

LAUDS

Across the orange eye
of the sun a thousand cranes
prefixed on morning.

Singing their hoarse praise,
they leap in ancient dances.
Altar-drawn, they rise.

PRIME

The cranes of morning
are a prayer wanting to fly.
They meditate the wind

until bone-warm, they
leap. Gray ghosts, air's aspirates,
God's sighs. They soar.

Earth's pristine scripture
engraved upon the skies. Palms
with wings, they rise.

TERCE

In Day's gaping mouth
the tongues of trees are silent.
How empty heaven.

Corn crones, breaths of wind;
abandoned harps played by hands
invisible.

Sentinels of cranes
sleep the tuck of wing-held dreams.
Late morning. Quiet.

Who will strike the sun,
mute orange note, distant gong,
its vibrance folded?

SEXT

On a hill, a bull
shoulders time's antiquities:
blue, cloud. The noon sun

burns into the runes
of cranes. In a cave in France
a wall-figure dances

smoke's old mysteries.
Invisible stars wheel and
turn in bones, bull, bird.

Heaven dresses earth
in its cope of praise. Richly
it falls from the bull,

gathers its crimson
on the crowns of cranes;
river its silk lining.

NONES

Three. The cardinal
moment of the afternoon.
Sun's germ. Rudiment

of seed, bud, psalm.
Light sings through western rose, red
rims sedge, spills itself

on box-wood, granite:
cathedral-thurifer, earth,
mountain, grass, glass, lead:

Inordinate gift.
Sunlit cycles closing in
a scarlet crown.

VESPERS

Never catch the sun,
white hole in deepening blue:
pale moon, paler snow.

Can this hour be raised?
Black birds cross against dead sky,
split harsh tongues, goodbyes.

Hesperus. Whispers.
Pallidus. The penitential
clouds decline the moon.

COMPLINE

Night, river, down, egg;
darkness on lucent darkness:
love's incubation.

The water willows,
the moon shines, weaves cranes into
the loom of time.

MATINS

The river's dark and
Iliat fingers twist away:
Oremus. . . . Amen.

From IN THE FIELD'S HANDS (1998)

JANUARY

This is a time of snow dreams,
of fox-thoughts loping across white fields,
of cold winds cleaning out our tongues,
the death of weak dictions.

This is a time when light,
like a crystal, fractures the sun,
waving it like a cold intricate fan
or a pheasant's plume.

A time when we love to hunt,
in which our eyes, full-bore,
empty the chambers of our heads,
scouring dull riflings.

So we walk. We let our boots
and shoulders talk, as if silence
were a charm, a little luck,
as if one word were way too much.

MARCH

Come, south wind,
warm palm and pulse of crane time.
Sage the winds.
Turn our solitude inside out.

Return the knots of ice
to what they were at birth,
beads of hope,
clear mysteries of unwordable water.
To what the clods and stalks
and pavements drink.

Come, purge us of our brittleness.
Make us adequate.
Be our aqueduct to spring.

APRIL

Let us sit down when
the dark greets the light,
when March meets May
with its souvenirs of winter;

when the yellow jonquils
offer the chalices of themselves,
and the wind's still filled
with ache.

Let us lie down when day
turns towards night's bed,
our voices no fencings
but a blend.

Let settle on your pillow
my gravest head.
We two are one,
and one with these.

SEPTEMBER

The month of bittersweet,
of orange gemmed with scarlet berries.
The month of cattails picked and varnished,
the holding on to summer.

My father driving the dirt roads of the county,
my mother with her English garden eyes.
What could be cut, she loved,
all those ochres and those umbers.

The quick slice of his pocket knife,
on her bare tables the tenacities
of her dry bouquets. All fall
the bittersweet burned on,

small suns in a time
of grays and browns and duns.

From THE PLAIN SENSE OF THINGS
(1999)

HOME TO YOUR HOME PLACE

—for Larry Holland, 1937-1999

The cranes have come again in slow wheeling
haloes to your land. Riding the modulations
of the wind, they sing ghost songs,
and in your river every sandbar heads downstream.

Only those born to make the ground native
know how to handle light. Today, as I drive
your river road, the sky is peppered with wild voices,
the morning salted with your love.

Some men are, and what they are draws on
every aquifer of notice. To the east
your cottonwoods hang on in love.
To the west cranes fly up like syllables of smoke.

But wherever you are, the dark is turning light,
and swallows, white and blue, skim your river.
There, in that great orange sound that is the sun,
the gravity of their lightness dazzles you.

From INKLINGS (2001)

TWO HORSES

Two horses
standing on a rise
have just broken
a cast of night,
are a severity
of shoulders.

The light cannot
believe itself.

It can only
follow them down
into a swale,
among the redroot,
the nimblewill.

DROUGHT

Nothing cuts distance like a fence.
The dust, strung taut as wire,
hums sterile songs. The posts
of moments, dried and gnarled, dig in.

Grief tamps them down, walks on,
sliding its hand along the barbs.
In the sluffed dirt, the prints of boots
hang on, signatures of strain

and thin-lipped laughter. Lips crack
and break. There are soul cleats
on our tongues, salt cells
in the wounds of sepia weather.

THE WILDFIRE

Running over the prairie,
the wildfire was a red buffalo
remembering a once fenceless world.

Wind was stampeding the herd,
and dry grass was giving itself
like history.

Twenty feet high, the herd
was shifting and weaving,
the burnt black selves

of the old ones wisps of smoke,
ghosts of tallow after the wicks
had gone out.

And all across the landscape
there was a luminous dust.
While in the distance

the wildfire ran on,
a galloping sun,
a consuming crimson;

in the dry heat of the morning
an airy blood.

AN ACRE OF BUTTERFLIES

The Impressionists
never painted
with these yellows,

and couples
never flew with
such light grace.

The blooms
of the alfalfa
are astounded

by the aerial exclamations
on their page.

THE SHUNNING

> —*in rural Iowa*

As if the air were skin
that was constantly moving away,
as if his own flesh
were a misfitting covered with boils,
everywhere he turned there was
a scattering of members.
He went into fields,
and the fields wouldn't form.
His wife and daughters left him,
his hands wounded metals,
he brooded wet wood.
Even the sweet air would not
sing him home.

*

The members of the congregation
had become a carcass
with long arms and claws
that were a brilliant scarlet.
The head of the congregation
resembled a badger's,
with the exception of its ears,
which were a dog's.
The teeth of the congregation
were of the same brilliant scarlet
as its claws.

*

As he watched his wife walking down the road,
knowing she wouldn't come back,

he raged against those
who had graveled the distance.
He remembered those nights
when they had ridden out on each other
like silk over cork,
those nights when their thighs
were small animals.
And he remembered coming back,
their bodies taking the air
in its trust, flooded
with visceral memories.
And the falling away of consciousness,
and somewhere the soft applause.

*

He had learned this well,
that will is an inept beginning.
He had thrown himself at the world,
looking for salvation in work,
and the night had come back
upon him like a toad.
Yet somewhere there were things to be done
without tails in their mouths; somewhere
there were undeclined moments.
He wanted to begin with such acts.
In the cold sweet air of inconsequence
he wanted to begin again, as a form.

ACROSS THE ROAD FROM THE CEMETERY

In spring the apple trees are rarely wrong.
Out of the puzzle of their trunks and limbs
come the answers of their white organzas,

their impulsive cells, like good, unable
to contain themselves, as if white not green,
were the truer print of spring, as if a girl

could breathe good ghosts throughout the trees,
or that between the sky and ground
white could riot into a soundless sound,

each breath a cusp, a burst, an ode, a consilience
of blossoms with the stubbornness of bones.

LISTENING TO A PAVANE BY GABRIEL FAURE

Sometimes when you listen
to a pavane the sounds

are like flowers in a field.
There is a little wind

and a soft sun, and nothing
is bound for the horizon.

When you listen to a pavane,
sometimes the flowers speak their names,

amaryllis and dahlia, linaria
and sweet william.

The flowers of a pavane turn
slowly in the wind.

In a world filled with killings
they offer you their petals.

The voices of the flowers
are ocher and umber,

the voices of the flowers
are vermilion and rum.

Sometimes it is like this when
you listen to a pavane,

the petals of the flowers,
their sounds in the wind,

amaryllis, sweet william,
vermilion, and rum.

AT THE ROAD'S EDGE

At the road's edge the snowbirds
looked like the heads of brown weeds,
activated clods, a feathery hopping,
a scattering. But as they flew,

their white wing patches flashing
over the stubble, their brown
selves invisible, for a moment
they looked like snowflakes,

symphonies of whole notes bent
to an old baton. But just as
suddenly, as if perfectly scored,
they made a white sweep to the left

and landed, hunkering down.
When I got to the store, I called home.
What was it, I asked, had I come for?

THE GEESE

Driving home,
my hands correcting
the slight lateral movements
of the car on the ice,
I forgot the storm
and came alive with the geese.
From a distance folded in
trees and dull hills,
a sentence of wings
came toward me.
It was late afternoon,
the wind was bucking everything down,
and I marveled at the geese
holding their V.
The point gander was true
to his long neck's motive,
the other geese caught up
in that instinctual axis,
that old red center
which centers each goose,
its substance of bone and down.
And right before me,
sweeping low over the road,
these hulks of quills
climbed the telephone wires.
But they said nothing.
The wind kept rending
the cracks in the car,
the latest tunes kept rising
and falling on the latest charts,
until I awoke
and considered the distance
my hands had borne me
by themselves.

THE HIGH JUMPER

Looking at the standards,
he closes his eyes,
imagining himself
a pure figure following
a precise mathematical arc
to the bar,

and everything slows;

then he begins to close,
whip-backed,
gathering speed,
shoving the weight
of the universe down through
his foot, his right arm
shot up in a victory signal
toward heaven,
his right shoulder suddenly liquid,
his hip bones thrust out—

then everything stops,

and his body, floating,
knows nothing more
than itself,
is calm, severe, solid, yet light

(what *is* the sum of the length
of ourselves?)

and stays that way,
with no time over it,
hurrying.

TO BEAR BRYANT, SOMEWHERE ON THAT TALLER TOWER

In innocence the lines of our palms
are never longer, the blue that the sky
brings to us is always out of our past,
and the most important rivers run out
of the smallest glands in our lives.
So much for truths. This morning
the neighbor's laughter spraying over
the fence makes each leaf shine,
while his dog, upside down, is wriggling
his back into the density of this world.
No ideas but in things, another old coach said.
This morning finds the apple trees in flower,
the sparrows in the gutter, and the big-
boned Slavic girls on their way to work.
And my neighbor's boy with a football
calling his dog in the heaven of his own backyard.
Bear Bryant, if you're listening, look down.
O, the way the football flies just so,
like a cardinal between the red bud and the pear,
over the sensual mouths of the poppies--
look down, Bear Bryant, look down.
It's spring practice time, and the leaves
of the dandelions are speaking long and longer vowels.

FALL, NEBRASKA

He wears bull's bones with hyacinthine curls
above his eyes, the weight of forever
swinging back and forth between his legs;
he talks offensively about his upper arms.

In bed, his headphones on, he listens
to a brutal bass for hours, then rises,
eating on the run. But 30 universities
are interested in him. Even the governor

has graced his palm. At night, when cruising
Main, that four-block, dim-lit thoroughfare
of town, the sirens come to him. His fever
climbs, odes on written on his glands,

the re-tooled motor of his Mustang sings.
It all started gloriously enough in Little League,
when suffering his faithful parents to come
to him, he stood in trophied grace along

the third-base line. It was there that he
accepted the United Way's Outstanding Midget
of the Year. Now a dozen coaches have visited
his home, the gifts are in. No tripods

of Homeric gold, no talking stallions, concubines.
These the NCAA denies. Only an athletic dorm,
un-spartan, and a chance for immortality on
some warm afternoon, the bards on high,

his helmet bronzed and blazing in the sun.
Fated by talent, public taste, and newspapers
which say he's more important than bodies
terrorized and dumped from jets, he takes the field.

A current of blood fury courses through his veins,
the outcome is knotted in his gut, the dream
of who he is, and was, in doubt. And who
cares if the kid himself can barely read,

there are better uses for his breath.
This coliseum's his home, each coach his guardian,
and this is his life after death.

A ROUNDBALL HOSANNA

King, right side to Graham, the shot
on the way by Siefert, the cutter blocked,
the ball whanging iron, smacking the glass
and kicking back, a reunion with a mythic hoop
which loops it in a slow religious cycle,
where time swarms, where on every mouth
there is the great long O of the jump circle;
the cheerleaders, like the ball, french-kissed,
(lipped up and out and back and in), the floor
itself like Eden's light, more precious
than communion wine or a saint's bones in
suspended time; the fight song in Icarian flight,
our sweat, like Heather's close and tight—
the key to a town on Friday night.

THE GRAMMAR OF BRONZE

—upon looking at the sculpture 'Athleta'

The aspirations of bronze,
the muscular clench and stretch of its flesh
to the point of its zenith. . . .

*

What is a graceful metal if not bone
breathing? Bronze has silver fingers and red
arms.

*

To have a body burn like a fuse
in immortal orange action—

every athlete dreams of this,
of being arrested in space, a heavy angel,
an endless tongue.

*

Here is a rich duet!
Bronze and its baritone
to the sky's coloratura soprano.

*

When bronze dreams, it assumes human
forms without wrists or knees, without hinges,
of something so dense and liquid
flesh is an extension of itself,
and like water, frictionless.

*

Bronze has no other choice.
It has to risk space.

TO A RECLUSIVE PHILOSOPHER

In that moment invited by the clause,
when adverbials turn golden
or at least as promising
as a remembrance of;

when time becomes replete
with the perfume of a hunch,
prefiguring close, and yet
remains a movement toward;

and when as thought you move
toward a house of independent means
where silence sets out tea,
has opened a sensual door

and waits voiceless near the garden—
you must declare yourself for what you are,
no footnote, but a bargain.

INKLINGS

When we first came upon them,
they were the smallest of all animals,
their tails pulled in
so that it was impossible
to catch them from behind.

The slightest wind blew them around
like dust balls in a room,
although seen straight on
they appeared to have human faces.

Half wore tragic masks;
others bore something vaguely
resembling a baby's smile.

We might have been amused,
but occasionally in singing
they uttered the slimmest of all sounds,
the lightest of all blood notes,
and we listened.

As if we were expected to hear them,
as if they suffered when
they could not come to completion.

A SONG OF WREATHS

In the winter, sing a song of wreaths,
the withes of willows, the ways of hemlocks,
the small fan-shaped sheaves of green.

Narrow velvet ribbons run through laurels
like the arteries of love.
In the winter, sing a song of wreaths.

Red carnations among the boxwoods,
cones delicately bronzed—
briefly, they are amazed.

Among the yews' tenacious needles
bleed the smallest of all rose hips.
Sing a song of wreaths.

A BIRTHDAY PRESENT

> *for you (whenever your birthday may be)*
> *is enclosed. Break a cottonwood branch*
> *at the knuckle and you can find a star.*
> *Now, my poet friend, that's a metaphor*
> *you can run with.*
> *Stan Smith*

So I slip the broken branch
from beneath the tape, and sure enough,
the star is there, wood's heart,
a little bit of heaven
between my forefinger and my thumb.

So how long would it take my joints
to grow articulate points,
and if broken at the knuckle,
would anyone pass me on as a testament
of would, or ought, or love?

From buckled, knuckled force
comes star-like love
and all its metaphors.
Stars in my knuckles make time click,
and my wrists are usually bound
to the sense they're making;
so at my age, when very little's
the real nickel, the genuine dime,
star time is. And nothing enriches
my wooden life like metaphor.

So, I thank you, friend.
Your one small star
is indeed a heavenly moment.

POSTCARDS TO AN APHORIST

Light is the only authentic.

*

Love is touch at its zenith.

*

Even in a necropolis a poet would write.

*

A present participle is a tongue with a continuing taste.

*

A resonant silence champions meaning.

*

And the last word on the edge of extinction?
What would you throw it?

NEVER WRITE IN A GLASS HOUSE

Never write in a glass house,
the least spirit dies for the want of matter.
In winter, barely vertebrate,
souls shiver in dry grass.

Like wheat stubble, they're reduced
to playing children of the lowest god,
and common's their tongue
which wants to raise itself to lilt.

Last summer, morning glories
kept asking where the sun was headed,
their fragile loves blue witnesses
to August's moments.

As we age, summer is the first to go,
then spring. What's youth
if not our bodies making light
of our spirits' shades?

From THE YARN BIN (2001)

FOR OUR GRANDDAUGHTER PLAYING IN THE SUN

This morning you and your shadow are one.
You never feint at it, trying to bruise it in play.
At the edge of our lawn you darken yourself
in light ways.

When you run, you have the breath of fans.
Feigning sadness, only one of you leans away
from the light. Someday your shadow may keep alive
your mother's shade,

or in sickness drag the ground with frayed edges.
But tonight, as the sun falls westward
through our elms, your shadow, drawing into you,
will warm,

and will do it lightly as a darker world awakens.

"WOMAN ON A VERANDA"

—oil painting by Lawton Parker

As the woman stands on the veranda,
notice the punctuation of the light,
its exclamations of white,
as if the sun had settled into points.

Notice how she looks west,
the absence of her daughter,
grown, and gone,
an infiltration of blue moments.

What does she remember?
A small girl playing on the lawn,
her arms and legs sparklers
in the sun? The saffron moments

of iridescent love? Now,
in the late afternoon, light greens.
There are small shudderings
in the limbs beneath the leaves.

The woman's blue,
the afternoon is white,
memory's green: each
a brushstroke in a single scene.

THE CRAYON EATER

Jolene Booker was
a crayon eater, the sneakiest
our school ever saw.
Miss Watson could be
writing ovals on the board,
and Jolene would slip
a raw umber or a periwinkle
from her oily box
and macerate it
the way a log goes through
a pulp-grinder.
Yang, yang, yang,
and that sucker would be
gone.

And at recess
Jolene in the swings
was an awful sight.
Pumping higher and higher,
she'd yell at us from
just below the clouds,
her teeth clotted
with rusts and greens
and burnt siennas.

But after recess,
after we'd all calmed down,
Jolene would sneak out
one or two pastels,
something like a melon
or an orchid.
Yang, yang, yang,
and those pastels would be
gone.

Which began a life-long interest
for some of us in
eating habits.
Why doesn't a food eaten
have any effect
on the way it's eaten
by a glutton?
You'd think lighter crayons
would be nibbled on,
while the darker would be
gnashed. But not Jolene,
she devoured every one of them
with canine gusto.

Grown, she went through
husbands similarly.
Had a brute the first go-round.
Emasculated him in
about a year and left his tattoos
drooping. Then
she married an accountant,
someone so squeaky clean
he used to change
his morning socks at noon.
Yang, yang, yang,
and that accountant
he was gone.

The last I knew Jolene had quit the Co-op.
A recovered addict
who could walk down aisles
with only a tremor in her hands,
she was teaching
at the Plainview School.

There is however

the rumor she was caught
in the furnace room
with fourteen empty crayon boxes
at her feet, and that
her cheeks resembled those
of a half-starved hog,
one that had suddenly fallen
upon turquoise, magenta, and old gold.

THE BOY

I know it's fashionable
to believe that poetry
makes nothing happen.
In its own small way
this is a belief
which comforts cynics
in their smirks. Or one
which makes old sophomores
laugh. Maybe the two
are one.

But I remember a boy
who once looked at me
as if all poets were sissies.
He was huge, with hands
like spades, whose brothers,
I was told, were felons.

One day he wrote about
how his grandfather died,
how he was there to shut
his mouth and eyes,
and I praised him.

Later, I had a letter
from his teacher saying
he thought the poem
had saved the boy from prison.

This is no exaggeration.
He wrote the poem.
It happened.

GOLD MEDAL WINNER

> *—for my father, first-place winner
> in the National High School Mile
> Run at the University of Chicago,
> 1924.*

Let us be with the best milers always,
those who move in a fluid world, muscling their wills,
whose bones are apparently socketed in water;

who at the turn of the century ran to school,
their hands on the buggies' boxes pulling them on,
their pulse rates, in the high-40's, up slightly;

who in the twenties traveled east to Chicago,
occasionally training on the shoulders of roads,
farmers looking up, all sweat and all shine;

past Shelton and Arlington, Nebraska;
Boone and Waterloo, Iowa, over the Mississippi
at Clinton, and on to Stagg Field;

where against the country's best milers
they drank the cold cup of fear, seeing in the hand
of the starter the image of failing;

where the gun, canceling out every sensation
but habitual form, made them elbow their way
to the turn, their breaths already like oaths.

Caught in the pack and spiked in the heels, they ran;
with their heads jerked back and mouths grotesque,
they ran;

with their lungs blood-red, saw-toothed like gills,
they ran; until light became hard in their gut,
until squeezed from the mouth of each cell

all the molecules of glucose keep bursting and bursting;
and from deep in their heads came
the oldest of voices, *your knees, bring your knees up* !

It was in that moment when truth became justice
that they ran for their jugular lives. As you did,
your eyes glazed at last, the light fading out,
when you took the last curve trailing milers.

APRIL

Visitors of color, the leaves are talking
greens on the thresholds of their tongues.
From the fields the cranes have almost gone.
The wind's assumed a softer vowel.

Last night our vane swung north to south,
easing the winter in our shoulders out.
Tonight my wife is sleeveless, the neighbors
opening windows, the mail-slots of spring.

This turn in our lives was such a gracious thing,
the breeze filling our curtains with good will;
in our windows' panes the breaths of the last frost.
Down the hall our kids kicked off their quilts,
their night-lights moths. All night they fluttered,
warmer than they had been for months.

THE TREEHOUSE

—for my children

I want to tell you
I put more than wood
notched with vacation precision
into this space of air,
the worst grains sawed out,
the early spring cold bothering
itself into my feet.
I even got my wife, your mother,
out of the house,
who then pulled up
on the ends of the 2 by 4's,
binding the saw.
But this passed,
and even the warped sheeting
of the floor relaxed.

And I want to tell you
the whole thing grew
surprisingly firm
before the two of us
went down into the basement,
bringing up little chairs,
a holey blanket,
and finally some coffee,
and how sitting up there in the treehouse
we toasted ourselves,
watching the clouds pass
north-northwest.

When finally I told a story:
of how Chad, once 6,
had to go Easter egg hunting

in old pajamas with feet in them
because he had the chicken pox
from sole to crown;
and how after all the eggs
were found, re-found,
and then again re-found,
I, in my arcane country wisdom,
saying no one could do it,
tried to break an egg
by placing it lengthwise
in my hands. Of course
it exploded into mush
and poxed laughter,
and for all I know
the clouds which were passing
north-northwest.

Anyway, I wanted
to tell you this.
I wanted to say it
from a treehouse
still here, still firm.
And how later on that day
the ham was good.

From GUTTER FLOWERS: THE ALLEY POEMS (2002-2005)

ALLEYS

Where the doors are off,
and there's an air which says, "Come in."

Where the only way's toward the other end,
and ruts of meaning last as long as frost.

Where griefs, like rocks, are found in beds.

To the left, chained dogs.
To the right, a mess of kittens.

Where rust is crippling every nail,
where odors, crashings, lose their fenders.

Where nothing's lost, and everything's tossed in.

Narrow islands, the ends of which are clear.

THE YOUNG WIDOW

The young widow has planted
moss rose in the drainage
of her cesspool at the farthest
reaches of her house.

Obscured by the pigweed,
it is rarely seen, so low
it goes unnoticed even
by the bees. Why, then,

using a corn knife,
would she cut a path next
to the seepage to look upon
the flowers whose centers bleed?

Consider God, apparently
like this in His needs.

WHILE LEANING AGAINST A GARBAGE CAN
BEHIND THE PRINCE OF PEACE CHURCH

It is Tuesday.
The ordinary kingdom has come.
Again the usual is spiritual.

So I pick a number.
Like One.

One garbage man walking along.
A bush green with the sun.
A church and its shadow in love.

And leaning against a garbage can,
I keep looking at One,
going in through the world of its oval,
finding it more than its sum.

MARCH MONDAY

The cold has got the mud tucked up.
Tire treads are hard around the edges
of the puddles, the water paned.

As the blunt tongues of the tulips
try to speak, a woman with her hose
below her knees is hanging out her wash,

her slips as galvanized as tin.
Red-knuckled, she stoops and pins
until her sheets extending from the back door

to a sawed-off tree hang in wooden time.
Her breaths, now hasped and pinned,
are riveted to her line.

ALLEY POET

Like an old dog
pulling a hamburger wrapper
through a fence,
he's learned to read
the taste of smells.

RUNNING OFF

"Come back,
you little shit,"
she says,

        her words
like a broken bottle
aimed at the back
of his head.

WITH FADED EYES AND A DIRTY DRESS

Wasn't she too made
to throw her smiles
like boomerangs into
a comeback world,

to watch them arc
through an air as rightly
fair, as sound as any
love has wrought?

Wasn't she too made
to be light's giggles
in the trees, a lilt of sorts
among congregations

of dark sentences?
What is there about
the wrong which sacks
a girl like this,

that leaves her standing
in an alley with faded eyes,
a dirty dress, her cheeks
a bruised redundance;

smelling for all the world
like hope gone wrong,
and ordered with her sisters
of abundance?

BEHIND THE MONUMENT COMPANY

An angel, one wing gone,
lies on its side.

There are no pupils
in its eyes.

What it's always stood for
is dead reckoning.

This morning a cat, curled up
on the stump of the angel's wing,

is making for it a poultice
warmer than the sun's.

Above them are windows
plaqued with dust.

Notice how the cat soothes
the angel with no fuss.

CINDERS AND HOLLYHOCKS

> *"An alley is a dump of bits and pieces connected by an air of disregard."*

No. An alley's still a poor kid's way to wealth.
No hopes are ever quite so crushed as rocks,
no black-eyed susans unable to seed themselves in
smashed-down fences. It takes the sun,
and an innocent angle of the mind, to make
coal gleam; and the discovery of old hex bolts
can thread minutes into moments. In an alley
no dead cat dies for those who cannot touch it, no
garage man grows familiar to chained dogs, and
even girls with deep bruises on their cheeks can
twirl hollyhocks between their fingers
and their thumbs, spinning them into rose-hued
ballerinas. In alleys every morning's China,
the chow with the purple tongue.

GUTTER FLOWERS

They flower,
and flower for someone
just by flowering.

In the curbs' cracks,
among the butts and condoms,
they are the future

chaliced in the present,
the case of a mood spun white;
thistle-less in the sun

where heat waves
wave like old Ophelias;
or run.

FOR THE BATTERED GIRL WHO ALWAYS SAID HELLO

Emerging from the fist of your house,
you came toward me like a sparkler
through the weeds,

even in August when the elephant ears
of the rhubarb fainted, and the backbones
of old nails scabbed up in rust.

Standing near your garbage cans,
I could always count on a fuse of orange
to ignite the goodness in your tongue.

You were like a lily in that alley.
One.

OLD COUPLE, PORCH SCENE

Why isn't the light lingering
in the cathedral of the sun

one hand reaching for another
in the name of love?

A DROP OF DEW

The clearest sense
of morning

among dragonflies
and bees.

FLOWERING PLUM BUSH

This is the way the snow should smell,
handfuls of aromas on black spines.

This afternoon a bush of deep conviction sings.
Spring is turning winter inside out.

Look: on the branches' long arthritic fingers
are petals of soft shouts.

PENNY ODES

The wag of a half-
blind dog.

Gleams of evening
in the gravel's tongues.

The last acts
of bottle caps.

Our mull-less blood.

The gracious pitting
of cement.

The smooth celebrations
of the shade.

The end of a run.

Twilight.

The total sum
of one.

TOO COLD

Too cold to snow
the old wives say,
the air too hurt
to cry white tears,
the sky too gray.

Who then brings
us these bouquets
of cold alyssum?
What madness
is reduced to this?

White periods
for the sentences
we cannot write.

Ends, like this,
which fail us
in our failing sight.

INSIDE BLUE'S TAVERN

Only near the alley door
is the air a snooker green.

Up front, among the ulcerated
stools, it's a rot-gut ether.

Shells dust the floor,
conversations lying among them,

and when you step on each,
they sound the same,

as if Blue had taken
the ligaments out of consonants

and eased them into drains.

THE MAN WITH A GARDEN FOR A YARD

The man with a garden for a yard
stands on his porch,
his eyes growing squash,
the air ripe as melons.

It's early March,
but even his terrace has been
plowed and raked,
each clod pulverized by love.

As time winds through his fence,
near the bird bath
new straw bales gleam
like ingots in the sun.

Checking his watch,
the man with a garden for yard
looks through his screen.
Dirt begins to tendril like a dream.

AT THE EDGE OF TOWN

Hard to know which is more gnarled,
the posts he hammers staples into
or the blue hummocks which run
across his hands like molehills.

Work has reduced his wrists
to bones, cut out of him
the easy flesh, and brought him
down to this, the crowbar's teeth

caught just behind a barb.
Again this morning
the crowbar's neck will make
its blue slip into wood,

there will be that moment
when too much strength
will cause the wire to break.
But even at 70, he says,

he has to have it right,
and more than right.
This morning, in the pewter light,
he has the scars to prove it.

AMONG THE POOR

Whoever talks philosophy in their alleys
is drunk on the elixir of big words.

Like gravel, what love is
is what love does.

Tough enough to keep weeds down,
hard enough to suffer suns,

it has a look beneath them.
But that's not true.

They need the dump and truck of love
to walk on too.

AT THE LAST INTERSECTION

Walk. Let yourself out. Be passed on.
A baton for barking dogs. Or silent.
Tickled by foxtail. Fluffed up. Quiet.

Past the shadow of your shadows,
past the hammered world where
everything's a bent-up love.

Hang true. Be plumb,
dropping from your crossbeams
through your breast.

If you must intersect with something,
try the sun. Eye level. On the bubble.
Walk. Don't run.

From WHEN MEMORY GIVES DUST A FACE (2008)

WHEN MEMORY GIVES DUST A FACE

When dust like flour sifted the road,
and weeds were skeletal corsages;
when horses broke their hooves unshod
with careless grass their only forage,

she sang high songs. And we listened
as we walked to town. No voice
was more enriched by pain. Her tongue
cleaved to love to make it new.

In loss the dust assumed her songs.
And clods assumed they had been sung to.

LITANY

Come to this place.

> We come to an old barn
> on a narrow dirt road past a church.

Come to old fields ripe with exhaustion.

> And a road which runs
> through the land
> and is graveled with syllables.

The hinge on the barn is an old tongue.

> The house is gone. A
> cave in the air,
> the house barely whispers.

Walk the foundation.

> We walk the foundation.

Speak the old nouns.

> We speak the old nouns.

Under the wind the dead dance in their circles.

> In reels the dead dance in
> their circles.

In time let them bring you around.

OLD IMMIGRANT

In church she was so quiet
it was as if she had the eyes of air.

In her rugged coat, bonneted,
taking the way with no stairs.

Past knuckles deformed by her cares,
past hands in which her veins blared.

Going up, up through the concentrations of silence,
through the beads of immaculate air.

AT FOURTEEN

To be shy,
to lower your eyes
after making a greeting,

to know
wherever you go
you'll be called on,

to fear
whoever you're near
will ask you,

to wear
the softer sides of the air
in rooms filled with angers,

your ship
always docked
in transparent slips

whose wharves
are sheerer
than membranes.

OUR ADONIS

Every summer he sprung from the high board
to the low one, then almost out of the pool,
his one-legged cannonballs the envy of cowards
and farmers with city brakes on their souls.
Even the girls pre-nubile grew intent.

Until that day as a wedge-buster he raced downfield,
the gold stripes on his helmet blurring him
like Mercury, arching him over the bodies
of three blockers, even beyond himself
as we had known him. And then his falling back,

his deadening down, the suddenness
of his broken neck astonishing the gods—
the helmet we slipped from him an empty crown,
his adorers standing, his opponents shocked
and, in their fumbling way, unbowed.

WALKING WITH MY FATHER'S SHADOW

Again this morning my shadow is his,
my steps filling out the ghosts of his bones.

As a kid with no car and no horse
he aimed himself at town and set off.

And sang as he walked,
The Bluebells of Scotland.

No wonder he became a miler who ran men down,
whose gait was like water.

Behind us this morning are our tracks in the snow.
Ahead the ridge clear.

I go, bodying out both fields and the air.
I walk with the shape of my father.

MET SOPRANO

The day my mother boarded the Met soprano
the paradox of her own contralto voice grew

lighter and deeper, the duet they sang a chord
of worth our house had never known,

the black soprano denied a room in our town's inn,
my mother in concert with a law which

ran back farther than the color of a singer's skin
and brought it forward to a woman named Camilla,

whose voice, in marrying to the richness
of my mother's, was not so much against, but on,

my mother's low register like my shoulders
on which the palms of the soprano lightly

held me down.

ZORN

In fishing, when we stood at that point
where the water runs from the river into the lake,

working the tackle into the evening,
playing out that monofilament from our palms,

you taught me how in strength,
strength falls.

In that sleeve of air that was ours
among the nighthawks, gnats and nocturnal turtles,

how to put thumb to the hook in the gathering dark,
and how in releasing the bait

and slipping the poles under our arms, we all
come back through the darkness the way we came,

our hands leaving little glittering pieces of feelings
behind us.

THAT SUMMER

As I sat dreaming
in that chair,
you came toward me
wearing nothing more recurrent
than the air.

THE CONEFLOWER

But it's beautiful, you said,
taking the wild coneflower
you'd found in a ditch

among loosestrife and thistles,
cockleburs and dock,
and centering it in a milk glass vase

full of baby's breath,
alyssum, and purple live-for-ever—
the flower you brought out of the country

gracing your cancer-drug table,
stalk-tough, its head up,
in its season a star of survival.

WITH YOU, AMONG THE CHURCH RUINS AT DEVENISH, IRELAND

Silence:
its invisible locus
and what it encompassed.

As it came over
those ruins, the stones embraced,
and the single lip of distance

almost spoke.
It gave breaths to myths,
to the axe-cries

in old Vikings' tongues,
to the prayers
in early churchmen's spines.

What it was
was love, and the glittering
dorsal fin of time.

ON YOUR BIRTHDAY, REMEMBER

Death cannot take your hand
from mine, nor mine from yours,
if our hands will not give up
what others call "the dead."

For some a remembered hand
can be almost as real as any
made of flesh and blood.
Just so your hand in mine,

brought back by love.
It's true, we met by accident,
but the intention of our stutters,
shy, ungrasping, was to love.

Now the fireflies on the lawn
are all the dead whose hands
are turning off and on. On pitch-
black nights, love is its own lantern.

JUST BEFORE CHRISTMAS

—at Burr Oak School

Eighteen below,
the cattle wearing overcoats of hoarfrost,
the South Loup River sending up warm plumes,
winter's cotton candy in the air.

As the school waits for the first pickup
to turn its working nose into the driveway
and deliver the first child to winds
which hone themselves like knives,
inside the room is as warm
as a big breakfast.

The teacher has has made sure each window
has given up its cataract of frost.
In fact, each window shines,
each student having signed one
with his name.

Everything is small,
within the reach of love.

The first coat-hook thanks a boy
who wriggles from his jacket,
unties the earflaps of his cap,
and with sausage and flapjacks on his breath,
says, *Let's see if the crawdads
have survived.*

In the center of the room
he lifts up tripods in a plastic pool
to see if every crawdad's home.
They are.

They're huge and brown and warm,
and like the kids, not one
believes it is deprived.

ABOUT EDUCATION

Imagine a village of children
in which each is invited to run.
Imagine them lining up in the sun,
in a light both strict and astounding.

And then the gun, which sounds like
the voice of a teacher, her report to the world.
Watch them run, their heads almost equal.
And then the line growing ragged,

some aiming down, others
with cramps in their lungs,
with those born to run having engines
for wills, their legs fluid pistons.

The point is they all get to run,
all get to express themselves in the acts
of their running: those who can't
get out of their blocks the non-starters,

those who run telling graduated tales.
About how one time the sun was both
strict and astounding, how children
lined up for their lives lost and won.

CENTENNIAL POEM

> —*for the University of Nebraska at Kearney*

Before the voters spoke, twenty acres yearned
to be small rooms past which a tail-race ran
with inarticulate speed. To fill a field
in which there was the grace of one green terrace.

The act once passed, its mortar formed a place
to which a hundred students brought their book-
bent selves, a study-stead for those who'd try their
minds upon the boards of understanding.

Around whom something more began to form.
Call it an education, that circumstance
still drawing us out, that thought-faring
that goes on when every page becomes a pulse,

each chapter one more verse, a turning
to new lives. Until we go by work, by words,
into the reaches of ourselves, the commencement
of who we were, and are, our fortune and surprise.

A REQUIEM FOR A TEACHER, STANLEY SMITH

Not everyone can be informed by love,
nor every word worn and measured by grief's
tongue. In loss the shoulders of the blackbirds are
    our sum.

Yet if flight is song,
the cranes will come again to tell us what wing is, and
canaries bless our cottonwoods.

*

It only takes two steps to make a rhythm,
one ear to hear a song;
and dumb by love, a mouth to find its way.

*

You loved good works because they cleansed
the air between them.
The air for you was such a generous house.

*

In absolute light are the hard still puzzled
by soft ways?
Like the wise, do they know what to give into?
Graceless, what is their rhythm?
How many souls make up the inexhaustible winds?
How many of them taught with their bones' chalk?
What are the givens?

*

Now the river bends in the curves of its dark arms.
Wherever its deeper currents run,
the wind is weeping light,
and the evening catches on whatever waves.

*

Is death that breath we hold inside ourselves until
it lips into the sun?
Like love, does it take us to the edge,
and just beyond?
Like a line of cranes in its ellipsis?

*

Morning. The river runs,
and with it the incoherence of its foam.
As light burnishes everything you loved,
your shadow, smokeless, stays upon our tongues.

DISTANCE

We are near, distance,
we are old and near.

We step more slowly,
our peripheries gauzy.

Dying is a drag on our eyes,
it is a kneeling of shoulders.

When we can't remember.
When, still, we come.

When the air embers,
burning our shadows.

When the light smokes
in our blood.

DEATH

Which cannot trumpet itself,
which cannot know if it lingers.

Which is the best thing
nothing has known.

Nothing, which is almost always
tainted with wrongs.

  *

And to think we put it in holes,
tamping it down,

where the heart of its heart,
its innocent note,

is no longer purer than
zeroes.

  *

Death,

who thinks he's the Big Boy,

who cannot even run things
alone.

NEAR THE END OF HIS LIFE

Near the end of his life
Aquinas looked at his work and found
only the image of straw,

chaff that shone like the sun,
gold so porous it held God's mind
like a sieve.

His bread lay on his plate,
his wine was a dark eye in his cup,
his meal, unutterable love.

What he had tried,
only in age to become quiet,
was to describe that clearing called God.

TO FIND ME

To find me
go to the park
with a bag of popcorn.

I'll be one of the pigeons.

From TRAVELS (2010)

THE PROMPTING OF A POEM

The prompting of a poem
has asked me to be humble

It has taught me to leave
all my shadows at its door

Saying it needs a voice
to help it out   that my moving in

will be its opening up
to ghosts that rise and fall

to whistles   pains   and small
clear windows

The prompting of a poem has promised me
I'll wake up somewhere else

TO A CARDINAL

—Clear Lake, Minnesota

When you finished singing
silence dropped like

a plumb line through
the wreckage of our lives

holding us still
as our blood ran on

asking us to be true
to the moment

As silence measured us up
making us as taut

as the string
from which it hung

more sensitive than
our weight had ever been

we were both equal to
and true

That morning   on the edge
of another winter

we were you

ELEGY FOR THE END OF MOTION

—west of Jackson Hole, Wyoming

His hammer could be as subtle as his words
his assertive voice registered with songs
his sports reflected on

As well as the long shelf of his life in books
whose margins bore his age in pencil

Now his shadow's gone
one proof of how he made his stands

But not his words   those settlements
he raised with his good mind

And his voice?   You'll find it
in these cleared-out woods

It's here he worked from peace a silence
like white nights

LYMAN LAKE, ARIZONA

As one by one the stations of the heat
went off the air

the horse of the dark lowered
the head of itself

and began to drink from this mirror

MONTANA SKY

In this blue
this blue in its blue-flood

in this free-up
without a black bird

there is only the moon
a slice of time

the silver tongue
of a bird

AFTER HAYING

There were evenings when
the land drew the sky across its pelvis

blue coming down
marrying the brown

filling the windbreaks
with the shadows of soft songs

IN TURNER'S FIELD

There were moments like this

when a small falcon
hanging in the air at the ends
of our breaths

was a commonplace stillness
that saved us

WHEN THAT SNOW DIED

—Harmon Park, Nebraska

That night when the snow fell
there were so many white voices

each with a newness of genius   each
an elf-flake on your lashes

Young   how could we have known that the cold
could be more than Siberian

or that in the heart of the snow there was
an inaudible weeping

How I loved you   your face turned upward
freckled with white

How I loved you when a million white words
were making sense of that lawn

It was like this   when that snow died
lace burned

FROM A VILLAGE IN NORMANDY

Evening   the last doves
are lifting themselves from the cobbles

Old women are beginning to think
of their hair as undone

A gray dog is loafing toward home

No wars   no bloody deaths
no mangling of bodies

Only shadows impersonating shadows

Every one of them sipping the sun

FROM TUSCANY

The air is full
but it is not depressing

Everything rising is full
of its vanishings

The lightest load is in the light

As each shadow hosts the nature
of its shade

the narcissus has stopped assuming
the history of its name

and patience is an angel
with no wings

JUNE, DENALI PARK, ALASKA

That morning the rain was coming down
in clear beads

its drops necklaces without strings

jewels common men might give
to their queens

And on the edge of that lake   a single doe
stood down shore from a woman
who was black in her grief

It was winter   for the one
in perpetual heat

BELFAST

That morning he was trying to find an art
which knew his mind

It was raining   down the street
a girl was dying

Early   it was a time
before the muddling of grave voices

before black figures hurt
the wet cement

a time when the water dripping from the eaves
was pure expression

when   like death   it was the only way
it could be said

DUBLIN

—remembering Gerard Manley Hopkins

Sickness has turned his world into a cemetery
but the man looking through the window is morning

is the pigeon flying up to him
the cloud bowing down

Is a weak man holding up light like a stray
like a lost-and-found instant

and the light   wiggling free   is running on
as a gift and not a betrayal

If all life is a series of vanishings
and memory a file of returns

between them there are moments
like this   this man

looking through this window   specifying glory
taking in the health of three nouns

From DELIBERATIONS (2012)

TO REMIND MYSELF

I walk. I put each foot
down in quiet.

I depend upon my legs
to take me.

To fall me into rhythms.
To stand me at attentions.

Until I don't obscure
the place that I'm in,

until I let some thought
remind myself,

until I let something think me
again.

WHAT IS A GOOD ROOM

What is a good room if not a stanza
with your name on the door,
a breath with walls,
the quarters of your held breathings.

Where, among charges,
squared breaths defend you;
where you put on dreams
that become you.

Not a tyranny,
not a collection of rules,
but an energy bent
by precision.

Where good work,
cornering silence,
keeps the air true.

REFLECTIONS, BEGINNING WITH TERNS

Then came the terns, extensions of the wind,
as if the air itself were tipped with grace.

That night, as they folded their wings in sleep,
the bubbles in their spirit-levels came to rest,

and the axis that turned that flock of birds
was a linear ghost, unguessed.

*

But the end of flight is not death. Can't terns perch
on clouds if we have the mind for them?

Can't their eyes, in rest, have their lives full?
At night, when the air in their hollow bones
is not still, why can't there be quiets

with the ghosts of iridescence?
In which something stirring, fills?

*

Slightly more than illusion, but less than thought,
Kant's bird was all wing.

Free, it filled without yearning,
enfleshed intuition,

like a hunch on a tongue
just before it could sing.

If goodness can be an urge found in nothing,

and beauty a hue in hollowness,

when can't truth be a lean,
an inclination so primary, lucent,

it's like that which prefigures dreams?

GRACE

In a very small church I remember
an old man trying to know grace,

the weight of its silence,
the clarity of its claim,

the lift in its wing as an elevator,
a favor to matter.

When he wanted was that moment
in which something took up

the rough sticks of his fingers,
flaring them beyond blood, beyond bone,

beyond the peg of his name—
transporting them

through the rooflessness of a thinker
who was not imagining a thing.

From TRYING TO REMEMBER LI PO

1.

The diamond of the poem
or the mountain's sermon,
which would you carry
through the fall?

15.

On North Mountain the blue wings
of a teal cooled the air.
A woman walked by, her eyes
lightly snowing.

27.

Since then it's been winter. . . .

50.

As much as we tried to like him
he kept kissing his footprints.

86.

Still, by the grace of night,
even owls begin to happen. . . .

133.

Another good morning.
What are you thinking?
Wake me to something like that.

155.

The bill of the hummingbird loses itself in the lily.
The geometer's line runs on forever in space. Here,
sit on this stool. There is room for two minds.

156.

Look, against this dawn sky
there is a moving sentence of swans,
one more love the sun can't burn away.

186.

"This world," Li Po says, "hates a thing too pure."
But the light, don't comb it from your hair.
Hide it in plain sight. I have the fingers to unlock it.

222.

The organ of St. Andrews.
For a moment the lyre-men put their strings down,
the goat-men with their pipes stand stunned,
listening to songs from the throat of a mountain.

287.

Stroke:
that cruel instead,
that knotted liquid thread,
that curdled bubble.

305.

All day we have been waving goodbye
to canopies of clouds.
I want to go this way,
slowly toward the horizon.

320.

Before me a drop of dew.
Which I take as a single water-grape of hope.
I raise my head to think upon its source,
while listening to the song-spring I have come to.

A SCRIBE

—for Art Pierce, at 94

A scribe is someone who bows
his head to letters,

who knows all the love
and exasperation in a pen,

who in appreciating the character
of parchment

has a hand that will not end.

THE ART DECOY

As he held it in his hand
they oohed and aahed,
marveling at the Goldeneye
he'd lured from wood.

But how could he tell them
of his rasps of love,
of his scorpers and files,
the fluting of his knives?

Or, under his glass,
how nagged he was
by the magnification of his errors
in the wings' fine lines?

How could he tell them
the decoy was nothing
like the deception
he'd perfected in his mind?

THE GLASSBLOWER

To an altar of fire
he brings not only
the offering of his hands,
but what he'll spend
in sweat and talent.

For what are his wares
if not what he plays out
from his lungs, his pieces
the result of inspiration.
At night, when molten glass

passes through his dreams
like the colors of his sleep
caressed by breaths,
what stirs in him
is not only the sureness

of his hands, but
the ethereal flourish
of lightning in a bottle,
the dream wick of
his liquid perfect piece.

THE BUILDER AND THE SINGER

—for David Rozema

Once, I parked my blunt truck
and, with my saw-tongue, got out.
Between the work road and the river,
I put aside for a moment my hammer

and walked wrench-less, thought plumb.
Then, when the sun was a drop
on my brow, I leveled the light;
and, in time, for a measure, tried water.

I considered the laps of the river:
tongued and grooved, how they sung.
Now, the hand that refined me
floating over that river holds on.

The one without scars and lost fingers,
that other falter and feeler.
Longer than chalk-lines, its songs.

IN OLD TOWN, A TRIPLET

1.

Here, every street-walker has a widow's peak.
The once-green boulevards sag.
Nothing is flush-cut.

Welcome, say old churches
losing their steps to the weeds.
Silent hang their bells

in their unshowered odors.
Nowhere are there health clubs,
nowhere are there stair-steppers

making their love engines lean.
In old town, where wombs have been
relieved of their metronomes.

Where all seeds are figs.

2.

Between two hitching posts in the oldest part of town
there is a low white stone which says Dunlap,
and from it a walk curving toward a porch
from which a ghost in white organza sends a wish.

And around the corner comes the apparition
of a horse, and on it a suitor in an immaculate
black jacket. From the porch the girl, demure,
almost waves. In the street the rider, dismounting,
hitches his reins to gold rings.

From the other world of flowers he has brought her
a blue lotus. And when evening rids itself of sun,
and the hand of Miss Dunlap rises like a moon
upon his arm, the two of them walk in,

into a scene no more interior than our dreams, where
everything Victorian, wick-lit, gleams.

3.

Invisible, she spent every evening on their porch,
waiting for him to come home,
their house massive, elaborate, its porch a wrap-around,
with worn steps leading down to gravel.

After her first and tragic birth, she remained
so clear no one could see her.
Once, her husband, picking up some dust,
threw it toward her swing, eliciting a gasp.

Appearing in the twilight was a pewter absence, her
shoulders bare, her waist no more mortal
than her wrists, the stems of which
were finer than the finest crystal.

Thereafter he came home to visit with her,
once bringing her a verse, a little ink of worth.
And for hours they talked, the cranes flying
over them like high, bodiless voices,
each one intent on stroking the air
and the ghost it had before it.

LOOKING AT AN OLD PHOTO, THROUGH SEPIA

Here they are again, all here, all hers,
all six dressed in her best,
the woman who rubbed her hours into fires,
who ignited the sticks of her wrists,
flashing out of herself the old alphas.

But that slash of light in her eye?
An old love wound? Her secret caesarean?
Note how out of this trunk and into the light
it suddenly knifes again in the open.

This woman who inched toward completion,
who loved love through its seasons,
who bloomed when nothing rained,
always still, always up until,
the one who took pains.

AMONG THE THINGS THAT DARKENED THAT EVENING

Listen, you said, as the dove
with its breasts of sound
was haunting our linden;

and almost down,
the sun was like the book
you held in your hand,

Cancer Ward
by A. Solzhenitsyn.
It was September,

when roots were rolling out
their rites of death,
and even the maiden grass

spoke Latin. A time
when words were not
in the beginning

but the end, when
they were last chapters
trying to imprint themselves

upon the wind. . . .

IN HIS HAILED-OUT GREENHOUSE

After the storm
the old botanist put on water music,

glissandos for the crushed hands of the ferns.
Then, getting up, he wandered through the ruins,

humming notes so soft they were like the tears
of moss or the breaths of crucified alyssum.

All afternoon, stumbling among pots and flats, he
tried to bring back instruments of plants,

until near evening he heard the cusp
of one green sound,

until he heard an inclination of new music
over the raw and angry ground.

MOWING

Today I mowed the lawn,
hunching myself to the task, the blade
under the machine whirring faster
than my combustible thoughts, faster

than the sparrow through the great hall
of the Saxon king, its wings whirring
over the mead cups, the savaged roasts,
the great man's queen and mastiff.

But at 77 I wanted a slower go,
something like our old elm cut down,
whose roots had given in for years,
adding to our lawn a slight depression.

Something like a grave into which
walkers like myself might go.
In the earth an understanding,
in the grass almost a door.

From ENDINGS

iii

What we assumed all summer
is not here. It's gone.

Like the light from a nebula
that for years kept coming on,
it quit.

A part of what we thought belonged
just stopped without a flare.

What was, was done, was spent;
a gift we couldn't pawn.

I'd like to tell you what it was,
but can't.   A sense? A song?
An ease?   A settledness?

A worn-out piece of long?

What we assumed all summer
now is gone.

v

Inside our heads
there are ghost houses
which we approach
across new-fallen snow.

There is no wind,
and we provide the sun.
And if a house is gone, we
walk its old foundations.

And we listen,
we listen for a tongue,
a name, a noun, until
a voice of consequence

comes back.
Someone who in singing
sings us into the sung. There
is a house

called love
inside our heads.
Greener in winter,
its dancers are the dead.

vi

—after an old song

But with spring in our flesh
the cranes come back,
funneling into a north
cold and black.

And we go out to them,
go out into the town,
welcoming them with
shouts, asking them down.

The winter flies away
when the cranes cross.
It falls into the north,
homeward and lost.

Let no one call it back
when the cranes fly,
silver birds, red-capped,
down the long sky.

IN TIMES OF CONSIDERABLE WARS
and INTERLUDES (2013)

You ask, is it true that only Nothing
  cannot be known as something else?

That on the other side of its falls
  there are no sparrows?

NEAR THE END OF OUR LONG WAR

—remembering Troy

How long do we have to stay hunched
in this horse?

In their houses the Trojans dip bread
into the juices of lambs.

Helens let their breasts fall like springs
on starved lands.

There are good explosions of children.

In here the cold is a spear. This plaque of frost
is no shield of Achilles.

Only our aches are embossed.

Remember the bright eyes of our cleverness?
All's cataracted, smeared.

Tonight the moon comes in

and sits down in the chair across the room.

It has everything to say.

Once, while you were sleeping,
    I let my fingers pass lightly over your lips.

    They told me everything about south,
how clear birds rising from soft shores

              are more than material to earth.

FROM THE CHRONICLES

—Anglo-Saxon Britain

1.

Then the force went forth from Unglia,
over Ocean's mouth to the body of Norther.
Our king was killed. Our army slaughtered.
The force became flesh eaters. They had sex
like animals. It was what they had dreamed of.

2.

On that day
                when the kingdom split
into five parts,
                when each of its senses
was shallowed, nothing
                      ravaged the land.
The force gathered
              in clearings.
Clots broke in the sun
                and ran.

3.

And Light was our king,   our uninjured reflector,
our unclouded sight,   our morning's soft sculptor.
We praised its deeds   as far as Dove;
as far as Horizon,   each of its thread-suns.

As far as West-stream,   rilled with colors.
Likewise Dusk,   as far as Slumber.
When Light dawned,   upstart it flew.
Our tears became sun   when Light was our King.

4.

Then the force came back from Wolfwin,
bringing with it its severe women.
Goaded by purgs and pukes of excitement,
it burned our people, exalting its gods.
More than our nights were injured into its darkness.
Each member entered an abbess, then slept.

5.

In the reign of No-Tongue's son,
Wordstun was appointed scribe,
a man whose inhabited initials
shunned the Viscerals' lives.

When Law was destroyed, and no plunder
seized there, Wordstun died.
He was hallowed to heaven at Worthchurch
where he lies.

6.

And when the long-haired star appeared,
everyone said a wise man would follow.
So we knitted a pall for him from the finest wool,
from Weep's sheep. Then we carved

a throne from the highest stone.
Which we hallowed with blood.
Every day we heard that the force,
those slicers of waves, were coming back
from Land's End, no bloodier hand-play
in their plunder.

                        But no wise man came.
When he should have advanced, he sat,
we were told, with others. And the force?
It multiplied like one hour after another.
It rode on more sea.

7.

At Marketdown the force fell upon us,
charging like words without grammar.
Which caused us to wonder:
how did the force goad its gutmen;
how did it forearm them for their kills?
Not that grammar defended us.
Before battles our counselors retched,
then vomited. Our best legends
were made sour by their fears.

8.

But when peace came again, we flowered our fields
with good weeping. With Succory and Holly,
Bee-balm and Pheasant Eye, with Hollow Root,
even with Nettle.

Our young scampered through Dodder and Madder,
through Brown-rape and Virgin's bower.
The old planted Lilium and Honesty,
Beam-bearers and Hunger-earth, Violets, and the balm
of good Thyme.

9.

Over the years a surprising character emerged,
one having the arms and legs of enemies.

Over a good cup this man would laugh,
seated among flowers fed by old entrails.

One of our storytellers said of him
that he had two faces on one head.

Not one of our dung-men believed him.
And as I write this, none ever has.

*From your cello
such moods.*

　　　*The hawk and the thrush
　　　in the same wood.*

Tonight the breeze's music is almost too light to hear:
*   on the edges of the violets are airs*
* for midges' ears.*

AFTER THE BODY BAG

> *—after Normandy*

For us the funeral was over,
but for them it went on,

grief eroding their years,
the topsoil of their pain

unable to find the silt
of a bottom; their lives

pooling and leaking,
an oozing of blood and clod.

Again that morning
the sun had come up

on the frost-covered grave
of their son. Like a tear

on the end of an icicle,
it was more and less

than a sum.

This morning you tell me
even the lily loses
  its prized tongues,

      and the award goes

    to silence.

              And that your dream is always the same.
            You are flying across a wordless distance,
                landing in a white hibiscus,
                    your tired wings outspread.

IN A DEATH CAMP'S MUSEUM

In here the dead move,
the dead move by moving,
the dead are unbound,

their bodies weightless,
cinder-less, trash-less,
full of the acrid,

their hands complicit
or charred.

It was evening, a time
    when dusk soothed the woods,

    when things faintly, gladly,
    tried to be good. . . .

    and we were walking when I asked,
        why is your sadness so unheard?

And you replied,
    those who speak of sadness
        must dress themselves in cures.

UPON THE ARRIVAL OF THE REFUGEES

—Rwanda

They fell on the ground
and gave birth to themselves.

They danced in the air
and flew on one wing.

When they talked,
they circled their tongues.

When they bathed,
the water danced naked.

As their machetes
lay on the ground,

the blood-red soil
loved the sun.

For hours their smiles kept fleeing
into their presence.

You said you would think the breeze would give up,
 but it doesn't. Right now it is moving among
  the barbarians, trying to peddle its violet skin.

                                Tonight, like the veil of water
                                        down the face of the dam
                                I will be a liquid journey
                                for your body.

FROM KOSOVO

They awake to bad mornings.

The breasts of the women have aureoles
of poverty,

the genitals of the men fall dead
on the ground.

Everywhere the air is necrotic,
even for children,

especially for children.
It cannot astound.

A moment like water,
*   like a drop of sound,*

with an intent so clear
*   it can be seen through. . . .*

                              hold one on your tongue.
                              *   What is it if not a bead of silence,*

                              a child of the unrung?

YOUR VICTIM

> *—Bosnia/Herzegovina*

I am with you always

The wound in your bone   the parasite
in your heart   your pussed iris

When I speak through your hand   the one
still over my mouth

my cries are misshapen gourds

I am the nightmare that wants
to burst your four chambers

The clot in your throat   the one
you can't scream

I am the vomit that stays
on your night-stand

the maggot that won't eat
your sick dreams

*A blackbird never
    gives up on itself,
just as a red wing
    is always bleeding.*

> *Here, in this thicket,
>   take my hand.*

> *No tower beyond tragedy,
>   the small lighthouse in our rock garden*
>
> *has one faint bulb.*
>
> > *At night it has a mortal sound:
> >   I miss you.*

LETTER TO AANYA, TWO MONTHS OLD, IN ISLAMABAD

Throughout the world
wishes shrivel on cold stones

or dry and crack
like disembodied blood.

Fanatics, especially those
with blunt-tongue tones,

will never love you
the way that universal well,

that source of love
can love you. Know then

there are a few
who bring this love

like water up, who drink
and are made whole.

This is a love which will ask you
to walk naked through the world

with nakedness your shield;
and long before

you understand the heart
of its great mystery

it will crucify you.
If those who know nothing

of its inner strength
believe you weak,

show them how love bends
iron to its gracious will,

or throws itself at storms
which try to unbone it.

In the fury of this world
there is no stronger verb

than love. It is the root
which lives through drought.

Aanya, my small noun,
may it find you out.

After I die,
*   think of me occasionally.*
*   I want to see the world*
*   through your eyes.*

Right here, in humility's snow,
your footprints are so meekly blessing themselves
*   they have almost no reason to go.*

IN A TIME OF CONSIDERABLE WARS

—Afghanistan

1. *The Corporal*

As he dies, his shadow lying beside him
is a good dog,

the sun still in love with his body,
as it's always done, extending his life.

In the dry light
the liquid rose on his chest

is a memorial to his dead lung,
while his shadow, which has never given birth

to itself, which has only mimicked
the words of his mouth

is a bloom, part of the still life
of a long afternoon.

2. *For Those in the Lame Man Platoon*

Yesterday your other eyes looked back at you
from their parallel worlds,

back from their rivers of silence.
You stood with them on the banks of your deaths.

They did not blink.
They were not measured by clocks.
If they were fortunate enough to age like clear panes

there was about them the fragrance of space

and the endlessness of good windows.
But it was no mistake they were born.

Their tears are good periods
in the books of the faithful.

3. *Overcast*

No limb stirs.
The trees loom space.

In this gauzy absence
nothing's a lead knowing.

So begins another week
of wrapped-up hatred,

its past and future forcing
our presence out the door,

down mud steps, past
two corpses, faceless,

the air around their bodies
unlived in   as before.

4. *In This Hole in the Earth*

In this hole in the earth I am reading your letter.
It is a soft hand, a good snow, a bird full of forests.

Because you are who you are, and I am a soldier,
I thank you for not taking me out of your dreams.

Remember when I told you there would always be
wars, that I simply hoped they weren't ours?

Now, from my living grave in this earth,
I hear fanatics threshing their nerves into screams.

On their chests are rows and rows of black
medals. I once again open your letter.

I am walking the coastline of history,
there is a blue wind behind me,

I am barefoot on your irreducible shore.

5. *New Snow*

I shall look up at the sun
until I find the face of it cloudless.

I shall reflect upon the eruptions
of its considerable anger.

I am small. No more than a sound
in a storm. No more intricate

than my beginnings. For what
was I born? From whose womb

was I uttered to be a kiss among
scars? A suffix of suffer?

They say heat rises. I shall try
to go up. I shall try

to make every effort to know me.
I must be considerate

in a time of considerable wars.

From GNOMES (2013)

After writing this brief,
I want to walk under eaves
where the icicles are coming apart
in the light's harp music of colors.

*

This morning the hawk of perhaps
is flying in case of, for maybe,
for the possibility of;
in an air almost alive with forever,
toward a plausible dove.

*

Two tire tracks leading into the distance,
far away toward the purple hills,

the green weeds in their center once

a bundle between a boy
and girl.

*

If history is a series of rivers,
why do you write about what's on this bank?

Notice the way the water interests itself
in your feet.

*

If poetry ennobles,
why does it move so few?

Even the light appeals
to every blunt head in the garden.

*

Silence is windless, yet it has an edge.
It can peal without a bell.
It can oppress without a cloud.
And sound though no one speaks it.

Tonight it stands here, framed,
as if it were a door.

*

Standing on one leg, the cranes
are entering their dreams,

in which something says *snow, white feathers*,
something says *wing*.

*

For him it was fifteen thrusts.
For her uninterrupted touch.
Midnight in the ballpark
of how much.

*

When Socrates asked, *What is justice?*
wasn't the light on the calloused hackberry

the same on the weeping willow?

*

On the mantle
the yellow eye of our candle
burns space.

Evening comes close,
a moth-down flapping,
not glowing.

*

Consider those like prepositions:
their almost thoughtless walking,
their flights without birds,
the rivulets of their minutes,
their little bridges towards.

*

In death our flesh goes dark.
But what of that otherness,
which sparks?

*

About your drawing:
this is the way to worship with a pencil,
the lines a mind makes married to a hand.
This is the way a hand holds within itself a head,
each small mark drawing from itself
the very thing it is.

*

That night when I went looking for you
beneath the street lights

all I found was yellow shatter.

*

Over the years the water in this canal
has left an inch of sand.

And you, what drifts do you have
in your word-bed?

*

You say it's necessary
to be dying.

I say, In time.
Better the notion

of your jasmine
than the raw side of this noon.

*

Every time I love you
I bring the future

into the present.

*

Having lost almost everything I am going to
    lose,

I sit here embracing my freedom.

The waves in this tail-race couldn't be clearer.
Today there are no better goodbyes.

From MORNING: LAST POEMS (2014)

ON THE WAY TO SCHOOL

Morning has no reason
to ride the bus again

after bullies beat it up
and split its chin.

But here is Morning
with its backpack on

in seat One again,
Morning, on the street

to Hell, a kid
of bright withins.

WITH GOOD MUSIC IN MY HEAD

I've known the childlessness of mornings,
the illnesses of souls.
I've walked with cancered tough ones
and navigated poles.

With cracks on sidewalks as my maps,
past academics, pinched;
when the sun's been cruel to shingles
and inch-worms out of inch.

I've walked through slogs of grayness
with good music in my head.
Bird-witted, run-footed,
I've been congenitally well-bred.

YOUNG

Young, we were fin-fliers, silver flairs.
"Come," you said, before
encrustations could turn us doctrinaire,
before we would gill despairs.

And I did. Following you,
I slipped nets, leaped dams and weirs.
What I brooked, my love,
was no more tangled than your hair.

Now old, we snorkel memories,
prolonging swimming in their light.
You, the one I've loved and confided in,
the long-haired star for my black nights.

FOR THE KID STILL DELIVERING THE GOODS

Southern Kansas. Revival meetings. Bill Kloefkorn.
Whose voice, baptized in words we call King James,
grew deep and long in lines so surely formed
they hang in air, ready for our out-stretched fingers.

What was it that let him feel in words both
a wit and wisdom, then let him finger them
into a music Orpheus once tuned?
To transfigure air into thrown song?

In a land where there's always a rock, a humbling stone,
one which takes Spring from our cock-sure voices
and throws them back a season, he was the grown kid
on the bike delivering beacons to our homes.

How he still grand-daughters summers.
And leads us north-by-northwest, organ-toned.

FOR SHIRLEY BUETTNER

This morning, in this world of disposable lies,
excellence pools.

A light without carp, one without suckers,
it moments our poor afternoons.

And you, still remembered by words,
how dark your boat, how narrow the fit

of its doom. But your verse?
Full of sense and strong waves how it moves.

So like this morning, which kept to itself
until it inhabited our rooms.

THE IRIS

This morning the iris,
fertile, deeply purple,
is presenting itself to hard woods.

But what can our oaks say
to this mystery of physics,
this propulsion of color,

this *esse* without words?
Now a bee drops by,
the transitive of a rooted lover.

It enters this oboe of morning.
It kisses its alto of color.

THE WHITE BLACKBIRD

There it was, a wonder perched in time,
a pearl-eyed thing feathering off into long wings.

What it sang was the last note indexed in the book
of silence. What it sorted was every sight

not related to salvation. And there, among
the split wood in my backyard, I let that bird

show me what to shed, silent as I stood there,
my axe in its white wind.

AFTER THE SUICIDE BOMBING

Gluts
of flesh
in the trees

and entrails
of black
blood,

where
breaths
had been

clearer
than
morning

and
had flown
like invisible

birds.

THIS MORNING

I found a feather in the alley,
so light it had not in its fall
disturbed the dust—

                                      like you,
just dead—

                        the down parts
of your voice still soft with bloom
and unfretted by the winds.

AFTER ALL THESE YEARS

We have become a good silence,
we talk to each other
like light and its beams.

Years into love, we have reduced
our addictions to words,
to those black and white fixtures

of pleasures, of pains. Silent,
we look to what's wise,
good acts for our misshapen fingers.

And we hold on, we hold on
like a drop of good rain,
among cruelties, inanities, gutters.

SILENCE, AGAIN

For years I've tried to map silence,
its islands of presence, its bays of absence,
the airs of its ethers and clouds.

In church, it lay in the folds of my hands.
In the infields of love, it was the catch in my throat.
Only occasionally was it a volcano

which blew through the roof of my mouth.
In the book of silence, its last chapter,
I'm still trying to sift the rest of it out:

the finest meanings of *silens, silere,*
and the unspoken letter in *doubt.*

THE PERFECT

Sixty years in coming,

it was the negative I'd tried to print,

and yesterday I saw it in a clearing,

in its finest hairs, upon a ground of chalk;

a thing without a scar,

in a time without a tense.

I had no words, no words at all,

for red fox sense.

From THE KEEPERS' PILE (2015)

IN THE DUCK BLIND

Blinded by the dark, we sat
gun-lapped, expecting ducks,
V's which signed themselves
upon the sun. Before dawn spoke,

when it was fainter than a wash,
I sat there looking east, the arm
of my father forearmed just beside me,
the wind not yet a pick-up on my cheek.

How small the things of what has not
escaped me, all those tap-in's of my past.
Like your finger's tip upon my forearm
before your full hand comes to pass.

ROWE SANCTUARY

—on the Platte River

This sanctuary knows its place.
It has so for a million years,
its grasses the original transcriptions
of how stems whisper winds.

And no one interprets this river
better than the cranes,
each one a long gray syllable
in the book of love.

This sanctuary says, *Come in.*
Wash your faces in the wind,
co-create wonder with your eyes,
treat your soles to something

other than cement. It says,
Worship is a natural event.
It's here you justify your lives.

PHEBE

One of those who healed
with quick precision,
her words were soft
with all the character of lace.

But there was always
a point to what she said,
and of such weight
it never suffered drivel.

What she abhorred were
those who reveled
in their petty pains.
Or fed upon the illnesses

of others. So at her death
we all stood mute, measuring
silence with our breaths,
as if they were the best

of else, and clearer
than words' tributes.

JACK'S LAST NOTES TO JILL

I lived for inclinations,
the dividends of hills.
Prospects were my currencies,
incomes to be tilled.

The ways I went were thoughtful,
into the biggest winds.
I tried to marry heart and head,
teeter-totters' twins.

    *

When absence is a flown bird
known only by its trace,

what do you do, alone in rooms,
encountering *agains*?

What do you do with old urges
just beneath your skin?

Ones like this, which jack you up,
to learn from hills again?

THE WORD IS NOT FREE

The word is not free.
It is ordered by letters.
Letters are not free.
They give themselves to words.

And sense? Sense
is free only to gather.
So, tell them,
that's why I wrote,

a clause in search
of myself, toward
sentences more
substantial than ghosts.

Tell them I bowed
my head to one word
after another; that, free to go,
I was ordered by others.

RE-LOADING SHELLS

The table where my father loaded
shells was no wider than a shelf,
his powder set to trigger storms,
his steel shot hard, like discipline.

It was a love which kept him
at it late at night, as if the dark,
once measured out and primed,
could have its life tucked in.

I'd hear him from my bed
bringing the crimper down and down,
each shell ending in a starburst
sealing some clay pigeon's fate.

I write this as a shell myself.
I chamber memory. It's late.

AUTHOR'S ACKNOWLEDGMENTS

Acknowledgments are due to the editors of the following magazines and books where some of these poems first appeared: *Aethlon, Arete, Axletree, Caduceus, Coachella Review, Chariton Review, Chernozem, The Ball State Forum, Blue Unicorn, Cedar Rock, Cottonwood Review, Epoch, Fugue, Georgia Review, Great River Review, Hummingbird, Identities* (Oxford University Press, Canada), *Laurel Review, The Long Pond Review, Midwest Quarterly, Nebraska English Journal, NebraskaLand, Nebraska Life, Nebraska Review, Nebraska Territory, The New Salt Creek Reader, Nimrod, Northeast, Pacific Review, Pendragon, Plain Song Review, Plainsongs, Poem, Poets On:, Point Riders Press, Pteranodon, Puerto del Sol, The Runner, Satire Newsletter, Smackwarm, Sewanee Review, Sweet Annie and Sweet Pea Review, The Small Farm, South Dakota Review, Southern Humanities Review, Tar River Poetry, Tendril, Wetting Our Lines Together, Whole Notes, World-Herald Magazine,* and *Yarrow.*

"The Reaches of the Platte River," "The Shunning," and "In a Time of Considerable Wars" are reprinted from *The Prairie Schooner.* Copyright the University of Nebraska Press.

EDITOR'S ACKNOWLEDGMENTS

The editor would like to thank Don and Marcia Welch for their patience and generosity; Jeff Lacey of Rogue Faculty Press for his immediate interest in, and enthusiasm for, the idea of the book; and Mollie Spieker for too many things to enumerate.

He would like to dedicate his work on this book to both his parents and his children.

now. As Welch attaches his broad vision to land and sky, birds and animals, he simultaneously tells us all about the solitary, bursting, and contradictory human heart. Born out of a deep and complex love, his inherited strength is transferred. Like the best of our American tradition, these are *spirituals*. Welch's beautiful and valiant poems touch needful readers on the shoulder, show us it will be okay, and, somehow, it is.

> —*Steve Langan, founder of The Seven Doctors Project, author of "What It Looks Like, How It Flies"*

Praise for *Homing*

"W. H. Auden once wrote 'A poet's hope: to be/like some valley cheese, /local, but prized everywhere.' This is about as precise a statement as one could ever make of Don Welch, the senior poet of Nebraska and of the Great Plains. Yet Don has always been a modest man, content to immerse himself in his first affections: family, homing pigeons, the Platte River and the birds that brand the flight path so uniquely, and writing an enduring poetry that never pretends to be anything but well-made. Those of us who have read his work faithfully for forty years recognize the magnitude of his contribution to the local, but we are also painfully aware his contribution to American letters should be celebrated in great measure. Don never sought a national audience. Rather, like the faith he has in his homing pigeons, he sent his poems to the world, hoping they (and not himself) would be prized and return to readers the spirit of the local that suffices above all.

—*Mark E. Sanders, publisher of Sandhills Press, author of "Conditions of Grace: New and Selected Poems"*

"Don Welch's ever-present theme—you are not listening for it, yet it finds you—is courage, specifically moral courage. And how difficult that is to sustain. Still, this is the music we have always needed and need even more, right

ABOUT THE EDITOR

DWAINE SPIEKER teaches British Literature, Composition, and Creative Writing at Wayne High School in Wayne, NE. After growing up on a farm outside Elgin, NE, he attended the University of Nebraska at Kearney, graduating in 1997. In 2001, he received his Master of Arts in English from the University of Nebraska-Lincoln, and twice has been the recipient of National Endowment for the Humanities grants in the Summer Seminars for Schoolteachers program (2002 and 2007). He was named the 2009 Educator of the Year by the Wayne Area Economic Development Council.

Spieker's poetry has appeared in *Plainsongs, The Platte Valley Review, The Nebraska Poets Calendar, The Plain Song Review, The Omaha World-Herald, Nebraska Life, Midwest Quarterly, Aethlon, Nimrod,* and *Prairie Schooner*. His first book, *Garden of Stars*, published by All Along Press in St. Louis, MO, won the 2010 Nebraska Book Award for Poetry. His second collection, *The Way Magellan Must Have Felt*, was published by Rogue Faculty Press in 2014. He was also a finalist for the 2014 Pablo Neruda Prize from *Nimrod*.

Spieker lives in Wayne with his wife and four children.

Don Welch by the Platte River, 2015

www.ingramcontent.com/pod-product-compliance
Lightning Source LLC
Chambersburg PA
CBHW050853160426
43194CB00011B/2137